COMPLETELY FOXED

COMPLETELY
FOXED

Miles Smeeton

Western Producer Prairie Books
Saskatoon, Saskatchewan

Cover illustration and design by Warren Clark

Printed and bound in Canada

*Western Producer Prairie Books is a unique publishing venture located
in the middle of western Canada and owned by a group of prairie
farmers who are members of Saskatchewan Wheat Pool. From the first
book in 1954, a reprint of a serial originally carried in the weekly
newspaper,* The Western Producer, *to the book before you now, the
tradition of providing enjoyable and informative reading for all
Canadians is continued.*

Canadian Cataloguing in Publication Data

Smeeton, Miles, 1906–

Completely foxed

*Previously published by Van Nostrand Reinhold,
1980; Key Porter, 1984.*
ISBN 0–88833–314–5

*1. Smeeton, Miles, 1906– 2. Wildlife conservation
—Alberta. 3. Animals—Alberta—Anecdotes.*
I. Title.

QL791.S64 1990   599.097123   C90–097105–3

To my only Beryl

Contents

Acknowledgements

I WISH TO THANK the Houghton Mifflin Company Ltd. for their permission to use the description of trumpeter and whistler swans in flight from *A Natural History of American Birds of Eastern, Central, and North America*, by Edward Howe Forbush and John Richard May.

For the information about wood bison, about which we knew nothing, I am indebted to the "Natural History Papers" of the National Museum of Canada, No. 8 of 30 August 1960, by A. W. Banfield and N. S. Novakowski, and to a paper on the survival of the wood bison presented to the 45th Annual General Meeting of the American Society of Mammalogists, on the 20 June 1965, at Winnipeg by N. S. Novakowski and W. E. Stephens. Beryl and I are particularly indebted to Doctor Val Geist and Doctor Nick Novakowski for their advice and support and to Doctor Drake Hocking CWS, chairman of the Wood Bison Committee, who entrusted us with the care of Martha and Mary.

For financial assistance in the buying of fencing material, our thanks are due to the Canadian Wildlife Service, to Petro Canada, and to the Elsa Wild Animal Appeal of Canada. We are grateful to various individuals who have shown their confidence in a future for the swift foxes by their generous aid; in particular, Jim Smith, Evelyn de Mille, and Betty Henderson. For keeping the expense of fencing down, we have to thank the many friends who came on their weekends to help put it up.

On behalf of the foxes we have to thank Agnew's Hatcheries, Jim Bruce of the Animal Care Department of the University of Calgary, Doug Buckle, for chicks, rabbits, and gophers, and especially Bill Rackstraw for his beautiful photographs.

Lastly, I have to thank Vivi Sykes and Sylvia Stacey for assistance in the typing. Particularly Vivi, who bore the brunt of it.

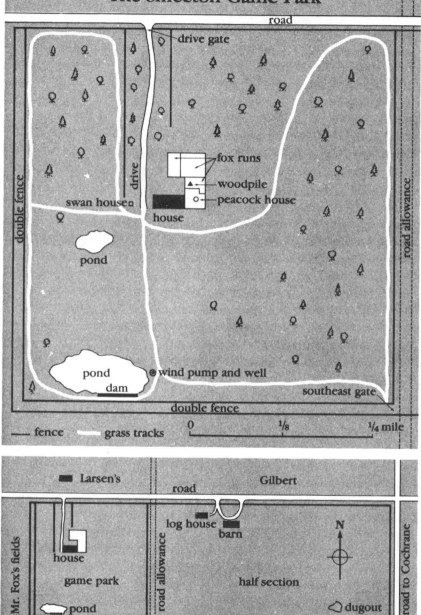

The Smeeton Game Park

road

drive gate

fox runs

woodpile

swan house

peacock house

house

pond

pond

dam

wind pump and well

southeast gate

double fence

drive

double fence

road allowance

— fence   — grass tracks

| 0 | ⅛ | ¼ mile |

Larsen's   Gilbert

road

log house

barn

N

Mr. Fox's fields

house

game park

pond

road allowance

half section

dugout

road to Cochrane

Gilbert

| 0 | ¼ | ½ mile |

A Goss in the Game Park

*"What hills are yon, yon pleasant hills
The sun shines sweetly on"*

Ballad "The Gay Goss Hawk"

THE SUN CAME OVER the Prairie edge almost as if it were rising from the sea. It lit the distant peaks of the Rockies and the blue ridges below; it slowly brought colour to the dark spruce trees in the game park and touched the topmost twigs of the aspens with gold.

There was no wind and no sound. Somewhere under the trees the moose were lying and chewing their cud. They would know, although perhaps a quarter of a mile away, that Beryl and I were up and about the house, their big ears flicking like radar screens, one forward and one back, as they picked up and interpreted the distant noises about them.

It was the back end of the year. A dead time. Dead brown grass sparsely fringed the slope in front of the house; the pond was already frozen over and the wild duck were gone; the aspens stood naked and still, and the scrub birch, a useless weed covering most of the open spaces in the Game Park, looked so dry and twiggy that it was hard to believe it would recapture the green of early summer. The sun, however, shone daily out of a cloudless sky, low enough even at its zenith for the downstairs windows to trap its rays and bring warmth into the house.

Everything was waiting, holding its breath for the first real snows of winter. Only a few days ago, the hawks had been plentiful, sitting on the fence posts along Grand Valley or circling to the lift of the wind above the low brown hills bordering the valley's eastern side. Ferruginous, Rough-legged, Red-tailed and Swainsons, nearly all gone now that the gophers were underground. We saw only an occasional bird heading southwest towards the mountains, its flight as straight and steady as the vapour trails of the big jets, which sometimes, on clear days, marked their high and lonely courses across the sky. It looked to me as if they were all bound, at different altitudes, for the same place, where the sun shone every day, the ground was warm, the grass green, and the wild duck from the pond perhaps already there, in open water.

Beryl and I were staying where we were. But there were many compensations for our doing so. The first was the interest that we had in the animals, which tied us effectually to the game park. "Game park" sounds rather pretentious; but in order to keep any animals classified as "big game," the government wisely decrees that they must be kept within an area of 160 acres. This area has to be properly fenced before a licence is issued to operate a game park, whether for private or public interest. Ours was a private park, but in it, having become involved by the enthusiasm of our daughter, Clio, we hoped to do something for endangered Canadian wildlife. We bought property about thirty miles west of Calgary and fourteen miles northwest of Cochrane, complied with the regulations, and became operators of a game park.

Amongst other compensations that the winter affords are the wonderful unpolluted air, the sunshine, and the scenery, which changes with the weather. One day can be gray and dull beyond hope, with small powdery snowflakes dropping as if forever out of a drab sky, with the mountains hidden, the house hemmed in by dark spruce trees and naked aspen trunks. The next will be brilliant, the snow sparkling, the sun warm, yet the snow not melting, a day when the sound of the mooses' feet on the snow is like the sound of swans' wings creaking, and the mountains are clear-cut against a cloudless sky. Who would want to be on the sodden coast on a day like this?

There are other days, when the wind will blow ragged clouds over the mountain tops, showing dimly under their torn canopy, row upon row. It is then that I can imagine myself standing on some wild shore and that the rows of mountains are great waves approaching, the snow on the fields a rush of foam across the beach. There will be days and nights so cold that even living has a slight tinge of adventure, when a stoppage on the road, due to drifting snow, may turn into quite a serious mishap, or one is beset by unseemly and vulgar disasters of freezing pipes and septic fields.

After days of bitter cold, the warm Chinook wind will blow, bringing a temporary respite. The temperature leaps upwards, and an arch of cloud hangs over a belt of clear sky above the mountains. The common cold is prevalent and horses start coughing as if the wind were a miasma from unhealthy swamps. Finally comes the "run off," when the brown fields cup pools of water from the melted snow, which reflect the blue sky. The brown grass, these azure pools, and the white backdrop of the mountains combine to make the most colourful picture that Alberta can provide. The kildeer can be heard on the bank of the pond, and soon thereafter the whistle of ducks' wings above it.

It was November and there was still some bird life to be seen about the house. Our winter visitors, the chickadees, who spend the summer in the woods, were back at the fat newly hung on the spruce tree in front of the kitchen window. So were a hairy and two downy woodpeckers. One of these occasionally beat a staccato rat-tat-tat on the cedar shakes of the roof, causing Beryl to cry out in anger. It had already drilled several holes in the shakes, but fortunately under the overhanging eaves, where the shakes turn back to the house wall.

The snow lay thin on the ground and the nights were cold. Kochi, our old Powinda dog from Afghanistan, barked to be let in as soon as she saw the lights go on in the bedroom in the morning. She always preferred to sleep out in a kennel made from hay bales on the east side of the house, from where she could keep an ear open for the coyotes and sally forth to bark at them if she heard their lilting chorus within the vicinity of the game park. This was Kochi's territory, and she regularly inspected its boundary and marked its limits. While she was young, coyotes never came within the game park fence, and we believed, mistakenly, that they could not get in because of the mesh of galvanized wire we'd installed.

Just behind the house there is a spruce tree, often well loaded with little cones. A small brown squirrel came there every day from his home in the aspens and sometimes ventured as far as the spruce trees in the front of the house. Kochi, if she happened to be lying near, always feigned indifference and turned her head away. When she thought that the squirrel was close enough to be captured, she made a sudden dash for it. As the years passed the dashes became less sudden and the squirrel bolder. It always escaped, although sometimes only by the length of its tail and, having reached a safe vantage point on the top of the fence or a nearby tree, scolded Kochi until she lost interest and moved away.

One morning I was looking out of an upstairs window when I saw a large hawk fly up from the ground amongst the aspens. It did a stall turn about six feet off the ground and then flopped back on the snow. At first I thought it must have injured itself by flying into the power line that runs to the house through a cut in the trees. But as I watched the bird, it repeated the same flight pattern, springing up from the ground and falling back again. I then thought that it must have caught a foot in some baling twine (a natural hazard in this country), with one end frozen in the ground. I went for my field glasses, and when I got back saw that the hawk was sitting on a branch about ten feet off the ground. I could see its long barred tail and white eye stripe. Unmistakably a goshawk.

Through the glasses I could now see our friend the brown squirrel. He was on the ground, clinging to the bole of the tree on which the goshawk was perched, and on the opposite side from it. My window was shut so that I could not hear if he was scolding, but he was obviously in desperate straits, unable to go up the trunk of the tree and unable to risk seeking shelter in the nearest spruce tree, lest he should be caught on the ground. I had barely realized the situation before the goshawk dropped once more to the ground to the foot of the tree behind which the squirrel was hiding. This was too much for the squirrel. His nerve broke and he scampered away. In a moment, the goshawk sprang into the air, made his Immelman turn at six feet, and stooped on the squirrel. I saw the forward thrust of his talons, the wings spread, and the head drawn back, as he killed his prey. Too late I opened the window and shouted. The goshawk flew away through the aspens, the dead squirrel hanging from its claws.

The squirrel might have made a meal for our swift foxes, had he ventured into their run, but their favourite food is the gopher or, to be more correct, Richardson's ground squirrel. As we could not provide a regular supply of gophers, the foxes were being fed on chicken necks, which we bought, and on day-old cockerels, which are destroyed on hatching, and which Agnew's Hatcheries gave us for nothing.

Swift foxes were our only endangered species. They are the

northern breed of the kit foxes, differing from their southern cousins in that they are better prepared for the cold, with their shorter ears, bushier tails and thicker coats. Once common throughout the prairie provinces, they have been extinct in Canada for years, but can still be found in the states of Montana, Wyoming, North and South Dakota, and Colorado. They were first killed for their pelts. Then the plough and the spread of civilization destroyed their natural habitat. Those that remained were either poisoned, usually by eating coyote bait, or shot by cattlemen in the old days on the range, for they cannot resist chewing on leather. It is said that lariats and stirrup leathers were never safe if they could get at them, and they have been known to chew on the flaps of a saddle used as a pillow.

Whether it is really feasible to reintroduce an animal that has become extinct through the spread of civilization is questionable, but that is what we hoped to discover. Very little is known about Swift foxes, and they have a poor record for breeding in captivity; nevertheless, we intended to breed them and one day release them in their natural environment. Had we understood all the problems and work involved in their care, we might have thought twice about the project, especially having reached the age when it takes twice as long to do a quarter of the work one was capable of in one's youth. We had only been able to get hold of two pairs because they had been in captivity at the home of Mrs. Vona Bates, an ardent fox lover, who lives just outside Denver. She was eager that these Swift foxes should be returned to Canada and that their offspring might one day be set free on their ancestral range.

They were now in their gray winter coats, only their legs being sandy, with some white patches on their chests and bellies. They had a black tip to their brush, a black spot halfway up and on top of the brush, and a black thumb print on each side of their noses. On this bright November morning, we could see the four foxes at the gate of their run. They were eagerly awaiting their feed and were close together. Two of them were standing up on their hind legs, front paws against the wire of the gate. Two were sitting between them, paws close together and tails curled round. They looked like the caricature of a college group, a rowing "four," posed for a photograph. Four pairs of eyes, alert and bright, were fixed steadfastly on the latch on the back door, eight pointed ears were pricked towards it.

As soon as Beryl lifted the latch of the door, the group exploded, each fox going to a position where it hoped to be the first favoured by a gift of food. Beryl went into the run and knelt down, calling each fox by name — Napoleon, Emma, Josephine, and Nelson. The foxes came up in turn, although the order of their approach had no connection with the roll call. In spite of their supposedly trusting nature, they were suspicious, crouching and circling, sharp amber eyes watching for any unsuspected movement, bouncing away, like blown feathers, if unexpectedly alarmed. Napoleon and Nelson, after a cautious approach, snatched the food from her hand, but the two vixens smelt her fingers, as if to thank her before taking the chicks gently. They went off to eat their breakfast in private, eating the head of the chick first, and then returned for more. Napoleon, afraid that Beryl might leave before he had finished his portion, urinated on it to mark it and then hurried back for another helping. The fact that he had so marked his food did not necessarily mean another fox would not take it. It was done perhaps in hope that he would find it less palatable. Swift foxes are very keen markers. Now that we have several running free, they mark anything that they find left inadvertently on the ground, particularly table napkins, which are sometimes shaken out of a window with the crumbs from the tablecloth. Gloves are often stolen and never seen again. A cap or scarf, momentarily forgotten, is stinking by the time that it is recovered, and during the night droppings appear at every door.

While Beryl was feeding the foxes, they turned their attention from time to time towards the west, and presently the moose appeared from the aspens behind the run. They were led by Petruska, pacing eagerly and licking her lips. She stood seventeen hands at the shoulder, and it was hard to remember her as the knee-high abandoned waif who had been brought to us three years ago. She had a very special relationship with Beryl, never putting her ears back to her as she did to me, but now she just swung her head casually towards the fox pen and moved on without hesitation, round the end of the house to the wall of the stony terrace. There she waited, just outside a door leading into the garage, where the food was stored.

Behind her came the bull, Peterkin, standing nearly nineteen hands and stalking in a lordly way, his head topped by a fine pair of antlers. He looked like a duke balancing his coronet in a full-dress procession. Although he was still in rut, his ardour was cooling. He had lost some of his fine condition and had eaten little, while guarding Petruska from the possible arrival of another suitor. Although he came to stand by the wall where the feed bowls are placed, he turned away and gazed into the distance, as a horse will do, looking at something on the far horizon or merely failing to interpret something that was clear to our eyes. His coat was almost black on his back and flanks, shining with health. His face and muzzle were brown, his legs gray. The spread of his horns were fifty inches, and he had eight points on each side. A good three-year-old head. His bell was broad and thick, but there was very little rope — the tassel that hangs below it. He too had come to us as a month-old calf, shortly after Petruska's arrival, so that they were of the same age. He had been caught in a barbed wire fence near Wetaskiwin and deserted by the cow. He and Petruska were from widely different areas, making them very suitable breeding partners. Their first calf, a cow, had gone to the Calgary Zoo. Now they had seven-month-old twin sons, Castor and Pollux, whose buds of horns were just appearing. The bulls were difficult to tell apart, except by the way that they behaved — Castor was the more aggressive and mischievous. When they arrived at the wall, they imitated their father, looking off into the distance with ears pricked.

When Beryl opened the door, Petruska thrust her great head inside, stretching out her neck as she pleaded for bread. A slice of bread, any bread, however stale, was what she liked more than anything. Beryl stacked the four feed bowls, one on top of the other and shouldered her way past Petruska, saying as she did so, "Get out, Petruska. Get back. Let me past." Petruska backed awkwardly away from the door, making a U-turn with her head and neck as she did so, in an attempt to get her muzzle onto the top feed bowl. The two calves pushed in between their parents, who, as soon as they had finished their own portions, tried to polish off what remained of their sons' feed. Both adult moose were very gentle with their calves, but as far as food was concerned, it was every moose for himself.

As soon as the feed was finished, the two calves and Petruska turned their attention to the salt, which was under the spruce tree where the fat is hung for the birds. The young bulls went down onto their knees in order to lick it. Peterkin turned, and stood head high, looking to the south, as if he wanted to show off his profile. He stood illuminated by the early sun, and its rays turned the edge of his coat to gold. My wife and daughter give their love to all creatures great and small, whereas I, although interested in them all, am really only fond of dogs and horses. Peterkin was an exception. He could not whicker for you as a horse will do. He showed absolutely no sign of any affection. He came to the feed bowl as if it were his unquestionable right, and at times he could be truculent and even dangerous. Yet when he accompanied us on walks, or joined us when we were cutting firewood, making bonfires or fencing, we felt pleasure at his attention. Now as he glowed above his family, I felt great affection for him, tempered by considerable respect. Petruska would always be Beryl's favourite, but Peterkin was mine.

The moose always come for their food in winter, in the morning at sunrise. However, a change in weather, a strong wind, or snow will upset this regimen. In summer there may be gaps of several days but we usually see them every day in winter, when animals and birds are stoking up in anticipation for the cold to come or because food will be scarce.

That afternoon we had intended to burn an aspen brush pile in the woods. Aspen are pioneer trees, the first trees to sprout when land has been laid bare by fire. They have a short life, and having first sheltered the ubiquitous spruce, which grow under their protection, they surrender to their protégés and tumble down. In winter, in an aspen grove, the sun lights up the gray-green trunks, mottled with black markings, and casts their long shadows on the snow-shadows stretching dark and straight, but fading before they repeat the tracery of the interlocking small branches and twigs which form a brown lace against the sky. Here and there the sun lights up the shrouded shape of a fallen tree, or a dead tree still standing, or a tree leaning against its fellows, riddled with woodpecker or flicker holes. Keeping the woods orderly and the trees healthy could be a full-time job; not that the moose care. They like to break down a tall sapling, eat a few twigs and then leave it to die. Because the grass over the fence is always greener, where a sapling grows close to the fence, they will sometimes reach over and break the tree down, so that the top branches fall into the park. The fact that the fence is seven feet high and the diameter of the sapling at the break is perhaps two inches apparently presents no difficulty. There are, therefore, always plenty of dead trees, fallen trees, broken branches, and dying saplings to be burned. There are far more than we ever manage to clear up, but this is the time of year for bonfires, when the snow lies lightly on the ground so that the debris of the woodlands is not buried, nor is there any danger of the fire spreading.

Peterkin appreciated a bonfire. He was particularly interested in the dragging of the branches towards the fire. This made him excited; he behaved as if he wished to contest our right to move them. We had made a big pile of dead branches, and Peterkin was using his horns on it as if he wanted either to assist or correct our stacking. He was succeeding in neither. Eventually his interference was making things so difficult that we decided to leave it. We lit the fire and withdrew. For a time Peterkin was torn between his interest in the flames and our movements, but eventually settled on accompanying us towards the house.

Beryl and I had often thought that Peterkin recognized me as a bull and Beryl as a cow. Now, as he had done on other occasions when Beryl had been walking with a man, he tried to separate us by getting between us and turning round to face me with his head down. His eyes began to roll and suffuse, and his ears went back as he started to bash up a small pine tree. Beryl, who was a little to one side, said that she would go on to the house and call him for some food. Fortunately, moose seem to come slowly to the boil, and we recognized this behaviour merely as his statement that "This is mine." Whether he meant "my territory" or "my mistress" I did not know, but I knew that he was telling me quite plainly to keep away.

He was so busily engaged making himself smell like a bottle of pine-flavoured bath salts, that I plucked up my courage and stepped quickly past him, and very soon heard Beryl calling him from the house. Peterkin heard it too and appeared at the terrace, smelling of pine and licking his lips — perfectly gentle again. I felt that I would soon have to show him who was the master.

CHAPTER 2

Alas, Poor Peterkin

A FEW DAYS LATER, on a bitterly cold afternoon, Beryl and I took the Landrover, loaded with stones and wire netting, to the gate at the southeast corner of the game park. From there we moved along the south fence, stopping any holes or runways under the wire. We hoped by this means to keep out the coyotes, which otherwise might endanger the peafowl. The sky was a uniform dull gray, and the whole countryside seemed to be gray and dirty, the earth frozen hard, but only half concealed (as were some of the tasks that should have been done before winter). Soon snow would come, drawing its gentle sheet over uncompleted good intentions, whispering softly that whatever should have been done, could now await the spring. A day or two of snowfall, which looked as if it might start at any moment, then the sun would bring purity and light, short sparkling days, and bright clothes and burnt faces on the ski slopes.

By the time the stones were finished, the light was already going, and we started back for the house. On the far side of the pond, on the new ice, we noticed a white mound.

"What on earth's that?" asked Beryl. "It looks like a bush covered in snow, but I'm sure that it shouldn't be there."

"It looks like a swan to me," I replied, but my thoughts were on tea, "Let's get back to the house and I'll have a look through the telescope."

From time to time in the late fall and in summer, whistling swans and, less often, trumpeters halted for a night on their way to or from the North. We hoped one day to have a pair of trumpeters and so were always interested. But we had never seen them stop when the pond was frozen.

From the upstairs window I trained the telescope on the white object on the ice. I saw at once that it was a wounded swan. I could see that its breast feathers were stained with blood. It looked so

11

large that I felt sure that it was a trumpeter, but trumpeter or whistler, it had become separated from its flock and forced to land. They are so large and the only all white birds, so that they should never be mistaken for a goose, although it is difficult to differentiate between trumpeters and whistlers unless they are seen together, or unless one hears either of them call. They are both protected birds. Since we were hoping to get permission to have a pair of trumpeters on our pond, we felt that this was an omen. A wounded bird had come to the sanctuary in need of help, and we had to do something for it if we could.

"I know that it can keep the ice from trapping it by paddling," said Beryl, "but if it's wounded, it may not be able to do that."

"We could break the ice with the dinghy," I suggested, "It won't bear us otherwise."

We pulled on warm clothes and took the little Datsun truck down to the pond. The light still lingered, and as we put the oars in the dinghy and tried to break it out of the frozen ground, I could just make out the swan's head and long neck turning anxiously towards us. Suddenly, it spread its great wings and gave several slow beats, but it seemed unable to get off the ice. There was something poignant and beautiful about the lovely wounded bird in the snow and the gathering darkness, striving for the freedom of the skies.

After freeing the dinghy and getting it onto the pond, we were able to break the ice by standing in it and shifting our weight. Once it was in the water, I poled with an oar while Beryl sat as far aft as possible, so that I could push the bow up onto the ice, and we could make a channel. Although the lake was frozen, the mud at the bottom was as soft as ever so that my oar kept sticking. It was slow and laborious work, noisy with the crunching of the ice, my exclamations when I almost followed the oar into the water, and Beryl's instructions about direction. All the time it was getting darker but Beryl could still see the white form of the swan ahead. On two occasions it raised its wings and endeavoured to fly away. It was impossible to tell what was holding it — the stiffness of its wound, or the ice itself. I had no idea how we were going to get such a powerful bird into the dinghy. We had brought a net with us, but there was one thing certain: we would both be soaked and frozen before we got it into the boat.

"Only about twenty yards now," called Beryl, "and we're going too much to the right." I pushed the stern round but the noise of our near approach frightened the swan into one great effort, and somehow it managed to heave itself off the ice and fly off over the pond. "It's gone," cried Beryl, straining her eyes after the ghostly bird as it vanished with slow wing beats into the night. "It's so low that I don't think it will ever get over the fence."

We were able to paddle back through the channel of broken ice, and as we got near the shore, saw that the moose, who had come to investigate the noise, were there to meet us. Petruska came a few yards into the water and pushed her long nose over the bow of the dinghy to check that it was Beryl, before she wheeled round and let us land. Peterkin, excited by the voices and the sound of breaking ice, had turned his attention to the Datsun. He had got his antlers under the front fender and the little truck was rising until its front springs were fully extended and it looked as if in another moment its wheels would be in the air. Beryl ran round him while I picked up an oar and hit his flanks from behind. He wheeled and put his head down at me. Hitting him on the head with the oar would have been as much use as hitting him with a fly whisk. Instead I went for his forelegs below the knee. He spread his legs wide but kept his head down and didn't give an inch. Meanwhile, Beryl had started the truck and I was able to jump in beside her. We drove off leaving Peterkin in possession of the field; a bad move psychologically but it was difficult to see what else we could do. We stopped to try and follow the flight path of the swan towards the fence, but it was now too dark to see anything. We tried again next morning, but in vain. It had obviously flown over the fence, and we neither saw nor heard anything more of it.

The stone terrace in front of the downstairs rooms was effective in summer in keeping the moose away from the windows and the sliding glass doors, but snow cushioned the discomfort of the rough stones on moose feet in the winter. We didn't mind Petruska getting up and licking the window, where she left frozen smears, however we did object when Peterkin tapped the glass doors with his horns; it seemed quite possible that one day he would break them. He seemed to enjoy the reaction that this practice caused in the occupants of the house. A day or two after our affair by the pond, Beryl called up to me from downstairs, "Quickly! Peterkin's at the glass doors. You'll really have to do something."

I slid down the fire pole, round which the stairs curve and which is our normal way down, and grabbed a broom which happened to be against the wall. As I slid back the doors, Peterkin, seeing that I meant business, wheeled and jumped off the terrace. I took a tremendous swipe at his receding hindquarters, missed them completely, and the broom flew out of my hand. Peterkin turned round and tried his strength on the terrace wall, removing a huge stone that we had got into position with great labour and had fixed, or so we thought, with cement. Bill Mackay of the Calgary Zoo had once told us, "If you are going to hit moose, don't use a stick or something that may break. Use something so that they really know they've been hit." I shouted to Beryl to get me the crowbar from the garage, and she gave it to me while Peterkin was still trying to demolish the wall.

I hit him a heavy clout between the horns and expected him to fall half stunned to his knees. Instead, he turned and took a few steps away, then stopped and bleated, a noise I had not heard him make since he was a calf. I got down from the wall and went after him again. He ran off still bleating, then turned and looked towards me, putting his big ears forward in a strangely endearing manner. I was much relieved that he did not seem to be hurt, only puzzled. From then on he was as gentle as could be, and in the evening I gave him two crab apples, which he loved and which sent the saliva streaming from his mouth. He appeared to have accepted me, once more, as the boss moose. I rubbed his brown nose and examined his head between the horns where I had hit him. There was no sign of a bruise. Next day the reformed Peterkin even tolerated his calves when they pushed in under his horns to try and get some of his feed.

On November 10, with more fresh snow on the ground, I went to feed the horses. The sun was just rising. It caught the tops of the aspens in the wood beyond the pond in a splash of colour, while the ground between was dark and colourless. It lit the whole range of the Rockies for as far as I could see with a rosy glow. All the rest of the land, except for the one splash of colour in the aspens, was still cold and drab. It would be hard not to feel happy on such a morning. As I opened the gates at the end of the drive, a truck drove slowly past with two men in the cab, both wearing red coats and red caps as is the custom here when going deer hunting. I gave them a wave as they passed, but they turned their heads away. I wondered at their behaviour while I was driving to the barn. I noticed the tracks of their truck on my side of the road, and then saw that it had turned at the corner of the game fence, from where it had been returning when it had passed me.

The horses were standing on a knoll beside the fence, and they galloped along inside the fence as I drove on the road. It seemed to be a game with them— to meet me at the gate where the road led to the barn, and to make it as difficult as possible for me to get through the gate without letting them out. Once I was through the gate, they would race me to the barn, on a fresh morning like this, kicking up their heels as they went.

I thought no more of the two men in the truck until I got back to the drive gates. Then I saw Beryl, and Newt Gilbert, who owned the ranch across the road, coming up the drive in Newt's truck. Beryl was looking distressed. The early promise of the day had gone and the sky was gray, dulled as if by some tragedy hanging over us, as yet, unknown. She got out to speak to me. "Newt says that he has seen Peterkin lying near the fence and that he thinks some hunter may have shot him."

Sick with apprehension, we followed Newt's car. He stopped sixty yards from the corner of the fence, where there was a "No Shooting" notice. Peterkin was lying, as I had often seen him lie beneath our window, fully stretched out, his back towards us, his head pillowed on his horns. He was only thirty yards inside the fence. The snow fell in light flakes, gently, compassionately. One big ear was showing. I called to him. There was no answering flicker. Peterkin was dead.

We climbed the fence. There was a bullet hole from a high-velocity rifle in his shoulder and we discovered later that his heart had been shattered. He could not have known of his betrayal, because he seemed to have fallen where he stood and there was no sign of a struggle. Beryl and I standing beside him, felt an irreparable sense of loss, not only for a noble animal that had, with occasional arguments, honoured us with his trust, but for the loss of another small piece of the good world.

Only an hour later I saw a man in a red coat walking along outside the western fence. I found a Volvo stopped at the corner of the game park and walked down to meet him. His red hat, his red coat, his trousers and his boots were impeccable — no doubt the very best that money could buy. In his hand he had a high-velocity rifle with an expensive telescopic sight. Round his neck he had a walkie-talkie, on his shoulder some field glasses.

I asked him what he was doing.

"Hunting," he replied indignantly.

"Hunting what?"

"Deer, of course."

I asked him what he did with the walkie-talkie. He told me that his friend on the other side of the aspen wood, which that morning had been lit up by the early sun, had a transmitter also, so that they could direct each other if they put up a buck. I then told him that someone had shot our bull moose that morning, through the fence and beside a "No Shooting" sign.

"Well that man was no sportsman," he said.

As I looked at him, only four hundred yards from his car, walking in cultivated fields, and covered with such sophisticated paraphernalia, I wondered what he called himself. I should say that he was a middle-aged and probably successful businessman. He did not really appear to be enjoying himself. I wondered whether it was not something of the Hemingway mystique that sent him out there. A manly occupation and something to talk about afterwards. A man of the woods, however phony, a rifle in his hand and a flask in his pocket.

By now I was certain that the men who had killed Peterkin were those that I had seen in the truck and that they were then in the process of "casing the joint" to see if they could get the carcass out. We found that the tracks of the same truck had run off the road just opposite where Peterkin had been killed. He had been shot from the truck.

A relationship with a wild animal is liable to be more painful when it ends than is a relationship with a domestic animal. It is so difficult to establish, so tenuous while it exists. Its termination, even though the animal has given no affection, may be heartrending. It was so with Peterkin, and we were to experience it again with our foxes, and with other birds and animals for whom we assumed responsibility. Beryl and I had but a dim understanding of the anxiety, annoyance, frustration, and sorrow in store for us when we allowed the tendrils of emotion to tie our lives to theirs.

CHAPTER 3

The Little Foxes

"Take the foxes, the little foxes,
that spoil the vines."

NOVEMBER HAD BEEN A BAD MONTH, as depressing as its skies. But Christmas was coming with its messages of good will. The foxes had begun barking early in December, December 6 to be exact, on a bright moonlit night. A single sharp yap repeated at intervals of about half a minute for about five minutes was made by the dog foxes, particularly Nelson, usually when the moon was up, and when they saw something or thought they saw something that they did not understand. (Later they began barking with four or five consecutive barks, a yap, yap, yap, yap for no particular reason other than to say that they were there. A territorial bark.)

Something was stirring also in the hearts of the vixens. They made quite a different noise. a squall repeated several times; a sound of despair, so that when we first heard it we imagined a fox caught by some mischance in the wire of the fence, or in the grip of a great horned owl. I had heard countrymen in England talk of a vixen's scream as an unearthly noise, and I can imagine that the sound of the English fox, so much bigger than the swift fox, could be alarming when heard for the first time on a moonlit night from the depths of a dark wood.

In the fox run, we had built two kennels and had covered them with hay bales. Each kennel was made of three compartments and had two doors — one facing east and one south, away from the strongest winds. If one entrance is blocked by an enemy, a fox likes to know that it has an alternate way of escape.

If the wind was blowing, the foxes stayed in their kennels, but on a fine, still day, no matter how cold it might be, one or two foxes would be out, curled up on top of the hay bales, or huddled together, enjoying the sunshine. In the early morning, even before sunrise, they would be out running about in their pen, playing together and greeting each other when they met. In the evening, shortly before sunset, they took similar exercise. On both occasions they were anticipating their feed time. In between these periods of activity a fox could occasionally be seen apart from those on the hay bales, as it walked about in a slow, investigative manner checking to see if it could find a chicken neck, buried and forgotten. The interment usually consisted of a few strokes in the snow by a fox nose, and was never very efficient so that there was always hope of finding something.

Nights, especially moonlit nights, were the most active time. It was then that we heard barking, excited squeaking, and sometimes a turmoil of horrible fighting. The squeaking was usually made by an inferior fox greeting a superior fox and sounded like a child's clockwork toy being wound up very swiftly. At the same time, the inferior fox would crouch down and wag its tail. In England, when I was young, to talk of a fox's "tail" was a social solecism, as bad as referring to hounds as dogs, but it seems more appropriate with a swift fox to talk of a tail (rather than a brush), particularly when it is being wagged.

They also made the same squeaking noise when one fox made a pass at another, either in momentary bad temper, or in an endeavour to steal some food. When a real fight broke out, it sounded as if a whole consignment of clockwork toys were being wound and let run into an amplifier. This usually woke us up and, in the moonlight, we would see a scrum, a tangle of foxes, rolling over and over, for they always seemed to gang up on one fox. A shout from the window rarely had any effect and sometimes we hurried outside in the hopes of breaking up the fight before a fox was killed. The quarrel was always over by the time we got outside, and what it was all about we could only guess. One pair, Nelson and Emma, had already been mated before we got them. Swift foxes were reputed to mate for life so there should have been no problem. If they had not already selected their life partners, they should have done so by January. But swift foxes are "an enigma within an enigma."

Nelson could be seen sitting with Emma one day, both grooming each other, and on another day with Josephine. Napoleon also seemed to be equally attached to both vixens. Instead of a dog and a vixen being in each kennel they used to all bed down in one.

Only after a bad fight would one fox be banished to live by it-self in another kennel, and this could be any fox, but was usually Emma. After one particularly bad nocturnal battle both Napoleon and Josephine were in tatters, and we assumed that they had fought each other, although anyone could have been bitten in a free-for-all. It seemed as if they really liked to live in a huddle with all the excitement of changing affection and antipathy in an over-crowded community. At one time even Nelson, who was undoubt-edly the senior fox and to whom the others had always deferred, was in eclipse so that we missed his authoritative bark. This lasted for about two weeks, until one day it was obvious that he had regained his superior position, presumably after some night action with Napoleon.

Spring arrived with its usual rush, and suddenly all the aspen were in leaf, the pussy willows in bud, the catkins out, and the new grass beginning to show green in the brown fields. Down on the pond there were all kinds of duck, most of them paired, and on two successive days had come a wild yelping chorus, as a flock of whistlers, in an ever changing white V, undulated across the sky on their way north. Most welcome sound of all was the drumming of the snipe, which reminded me of marshes and wild places in many parts of the world and set my feet itching.

One day I was talking to Sid Ball, a neighbouring rancher friend in Horse Creek who had come out here in the twenties. His eyes are the colour of Albertan skies, and his grizzled tough face, as pugna-cious as a border terrier, is stamped with long years of hard and successful work in this harsh climate. We were talking about the coming of spring.

"It's good to hear the snipe drumming," I said.

"What's that?" he asked.

"The snipe drumming. Listen, there's one now."

"That's not a snipe. That's a mosquito hawk and no one's ever seen one."

I looked up, searching the skies, and presently saw a snipe. As I watched, it started its dive and presently we could hear, delayed because of the bird's great height above us, the ululation of its drumming.

"There's one, Sid. Look! Up there. You can see him. He makes that noise as he dives."

"Well, you've got mighty good eyes," said Sid, not deigning to look up for something that he knew perfectly well could not be seen. "How are your foxes doing? You should be having some cubs soon."

The foxes were behaving in the strangest way. For the last few days of April, the two vixens had been showing that they were carrying cubs. We had called the two kennels "West House" and "St. Helena". Josephine and Napoleon, with no historical sense, had settled in West House, while Emma had moved into St. Helena. Nelson made free of both houses indiscriminately. On May 5th, Emma was looking slim again and was very hungry, but Josephine was obviously still pregnant. Beryl decided that Emma had had her cubs in St. Helena, but on succeeding days everything became confused. Josephine and Napoleon rarely appeared, while Emma, when Beryl came to feed the foxes, made short runs towards West House. Beryl thought that she was trying to lead her away from the cubs in St. Helena, but when she gave Emma some food, Emma took it round and round West House, making a clucking noise like a hen calling its chicks. This gentle offering was greeted by growls from within. Next day she was seen pacing up and down the fence, a thing she had never done before, and at each turn, in a gesture of help-less despair, she threw her head up and so far back she nearly fell over. Beryl was sure now that she had lost her cubs, but owing to the horror with which the foxes regard any opening of their kennels, we did not want to disturb them without good reason, and waited for further developments.

For the next few days we saw nothing of Napoleon and Josephine, although the food put at the kennel door always disappeared. Emma carried her food to West House making her chuckling sound, but never ventured in and eventually ate what-ever she was carrying. Nelson, however, occasionally carried food into West House, but on the whole he remained aloof from what-ever was going on, sleeping, as far as we could tell, in whatever kennel he chose.

Beryl had intended to open the kennels and take one cub from each litter while they were still blind. She then planned to bring them up on a bottle so that they would become imprinted by her, and in time they would learn to go free and to hunt, but would regard our house as their home. From them we hoped to raise more cubs in a degree of freedom that would make them fit for release in the wild.

As only one litter appeared to have survived, we now had a problem, aggravated by a heavy fall of snow, since we did not want to open the kennels in bad weather. On May 19, Josephine came out of West House and there were great greetings among all the foxes and much thrashing of tails and squirming on the ground. It was obviously a day of congratulations. Josephine's belly looked very pink and Napoleon stayed close beside her, licking her belly and under her tail. We decided to open West House the following day.

It was a fine sunny morning. We removed the hay bales and, as we started to open the lid of the kennel, three foxes shot out of the entrances, in a great state of alarm. When the lid finally came open we found six or seven cubs in the central compartment, lying close together and looking like a packet of Palethorpe's sausages. They were of surprisingly different sizes and Beryl, in a hurry to put everything back in order, grabbed two, a male and a female, from the top of the heap and carried them away while I quickly shut the lid and put the hay bales in place. All the foxes were badly disturbed and rushed round and round the run in their anxiety.

As soon as we left the run, the foxes came back to the kennel to discover the extent of the disaster. For the rest of the day we saw Josephine and Napoleon always with a cub in their mouths, searching for a safe hiding place. They decided eventually on St. Helena.

The two cubs that we had taken were put in a cardboard box and covered with a woolen cloth. They were two of the ugliest little creatures, their faces crumpled with complaint and bad temper, their fur so short that they seemed almost naked, more like newborn rats than cubs. Beryl fed them, after five hours so that they should be hungry, with Esbillac from an eye dropper. It was not well received but she got some down, although, like feeding most babies, more seemed to go outside than in. While she was doing this, she discovered that the female cub had only a stump for one hind leg and, since there was no sore, had obviously been born like that. Beryl wondered if the malformation might be due to inbreeding and rang up Vona Bates who assured her that the dog foxes were quite unrelated either to each other or to the vixens, and that there would probably be no harm in disturbing the foxes again to take another cub. We decided to destroy the cripple. The other cub, left to himself, cried bitterly until we put him on an electric warming pad, where he soon settled down again.

Next day we opened St. Helena. Napoleon and Josephine flew out in a panic, but Nelson and Emma watched from a distance. Inside, instead of a bundle of cubs, we found only three. These were all well matched and of a good size, their eyes just opening, their coats much more advanced than the two that we had just taken. We could see now that once they had got rid of their dissatisfied expression, they would be as attractive as any puppy. Two of the three were females. We took one and put her with the male in the cardboard box. As they lay side by side the difference in their development was quite apparent. Obviously they were from two separate litters.

At last the goings on of the past few days were clear. Napoleon and Josephine had stolen Emma's cubs soon after they were born, and Nelson had failed to stand up for Emma seeming to think that any vixen would do as a mother for his cubs. Josephine, already so near her own time, had been able to suckle them, although she could not have brought up two litters — her own cubs eventually would have succumbed to the older and stronger opposition. We had taken two of her cubs initially, and in the comings and goings after the initial opening of the kennel, she had lost the rest. In the house we now had a male cub of Josephine's and a female cub of Emma's, while Josephine, outside in the run, had two cubs: a male and a female of Emma's. Emma, for the time being, was not allowed to have anything to do with them. Nelson was allowed into the kennel and permitted to bring them offerings of food, which I suppose Josephine ate. No wonder poor Emma paced the fence and threw herself backwards in despair.

Now that we had opened St. Helena and taken another cub, all the anxiety and the restless search for a safe refuge started again. The two cubs were dragged from one place to another until they were eventually deposited in West House, where they had been born. Luckily, although during these peregrinations they hung as if dead from the mouths of the worried parents, they were strong enough to withstand the rough treatment.

CHAPTER 4

Louis and Louisa

"Then the moon came quiet and flooded full
Light and beauty on clouds like wool,
On a feasted fox at rest from hunting."
Masefield

WE CALLED THE TWO that had been taken into the house Louis and
Louisa, and we soon discovered that in every process of development, such as the opening of dim blue and apparently sightless eyes,
the first taking of a little raw meat, the first exploration outside the
cardboard box, the first infantile bark, and the first sign of play,
Louis was always a week behind Louisa, which coincided with the
dates that we believed the litters to have been born.

The eye dropper gave place to a small rubber teat and a minia-
ture bottle, called a "nip pet nurser." Louis took to the teat more
quickly than did Louisa, who was inclined to chew rather than to
suck, and who quickly chewed her way through two teats. She also
started to seek sustenance from Louis, whose penis began to look
very sore, but apart from this they were both obviously doing well.

We had to go away for three days and took the cubs to Calgary to
stay with Lorraine Milne, a gentle psychologist, whose husband,
Bill, a well-known architect, had given us so much help and advice
with the house when we had first arrived. Lorraine overflows with
kindness and every squirrel in Roxborough claims her as a benefac-
tress. Beryl knew that her kindness was controlled by an analytical
mind and had no fears that the cubs would suffer from overfeeding.
When we got back, we found them looking splendid, and after three
days absence could appreciate their growth. Bill, on the other hand,
complained that he had been neglected and was losing weight.

While we were having lunch before taking the cubs home, we
became aware of a terrible screeching from the cardboard box, and

found that Louisa, whose teeth were as sharp as needles, had attacked Louis and bitten him badly in the stomach and hind leg. We separated them at once, putting Louis in a small carton. On arrival home, he was put in a suitcase, and since he was sick and shocked, he was given a heat pad. Louisa, whom Beryl now decided was in need of meat, was given small pieces of chick, which she ate voraciously. Their new homes did not contain them for long. When Louis climbed out, he staggered about until he blundered into a pile of Beryl's clothes, where he curled up and slept soundly; Louisa, being more agile than Louis, tacked with grim determination backwards and forwards across the room until by chance she hit her box and scrambled inside.

When Louisa was a month old she barked at me from her box as I came into the room. A few days later she saw me again when she was outside her box, barked, and scrambled back in. Beryl called to her, telling her not to be so nervous and to her delight, Louisa climbed out again and came over to her. True to his schedule, Louis gave his first bark a week later.

Both cubs were now eating cut up chicks as well as Esbillac. One day Louisa showed the first sign of playing when she got hold of the end of a towel that Beryl was holding. The next day she invaded Louis's box and another fight started. This time Louis stood up for himself, and when they were separated each lay facing the other, their mouths as wide open as those of nestlings expecting food and each prepared to resume the fight. The excitement was too much for Louisa—she went into a trauma. Her eyes became glassy and she rolled over onto her back, her legs jerking. This happened several times to Louisa at this time of her life, and was always caused by overexcitement, and heralded by her hind legs collapsing. Once it happened after she had been worrying a rag on which Louis had been lying. It was Louis who she thought she was attacking. We learnt then that swift fox cubs start trying to establish their dominance in the litter at a month old. This is probably effected in nature without undue damage, but owing to the difference in size between Louis and Louisa we decided to keep them apart. Louisa and her box were sent downstairs. The separation of the cubs did not last for long. After a few days we put them together outside, in the sun and shadow of the aspen trees, amongst the green grass and flowers. Louis crouched down in front of Louisa, wagging his tail (or what passed for a tail at that stage of his growth), and chittered to her—a very humble little fox. Louisa, unaffected by the pastoral scene, made an altogether different noise at him, which almost resembled a snarl. Beryl's nerve broke and she snatched Louis up before he was savaged. Meanwhile, the two cubs in the run were seen outside their kennel. They looked a little bigger than Louisa and better coordinated but she wasn't far behind. Mother's milk was obviously best. When Louisa was outside she seemed to know where she was going, if not for what purpose; Louis, however, still staggered about, his movements as vague as those of a drunken man. They were no longer ugly, but woolly, sharpnosed, button-eyed little charmers.

When the "outside" foxes were fed in the run, Emma took her chick to wherever the cubs were living, alternating between West House and St. Helena, and ran round the kennel making her chuckling noise, as she called vainly for the cubs to come out and be fed. The others took their chicks inside to the cubs. Beryl imitated Emma's clucking sound when she fed Louis and Louisa, and they responded with eager chattering. Emma's unhappiness was not prolonged, for on June 18, outside St. Helena we saw both cubs being fed by Josephine, Emma, and Napoleon. Nelson, with the air of a man not prepared to be bothered by this nursery business, was burying his chick in a corner of the run. A day or two later I saw Emma feeding the cubs, while Josephine and Napoleon watched indulgently from a seat on the hay bales. Her ostracism was over, her appetite increased, and soon she looked so fat that Beryl began to wonder if she were having another go at raising a family.

By the end of the month the indoor cubs were both downstairs, but living in separate boxes when they were not exercising. They were given a little raw meat now, as well as chicks. They had already started trying to bury their chicks when they had had enough for one meal, by pushing imaginary earth over them in the corners of the living room.

About this time, Stuart Johnston arrived to live with us. He drifted in from the coast where he had been staying with our daughter and son-in-law, helping Clio with a study of the causes of injury and death to sea birds along the shores at Victoria.

"You really should have someone to help," she told us, "and he's just the person for you. He won't want any pay if you feed and keep him. He'll sleep anywhere, and he's just mad about birds."

Stuart was a tall, thin, but well-built American of about twenty-six years, with long fair hair, tied at the back of his neck by an elastic band. His manner was extremely gentle, and when he spoke his deep voice rumbled slowly out of the depths of a vast beard. This muffled rumbling, combined with a mid-west accent, made what he said rarely intelligible to me, although Beryl and Clio could inter-pret the sounds quite easily. I put this down to their understanding and love for wild animals, for Stuart was something of a wild animal himself, suffering the bonds of discipline and convention with difficulty. Above the brown bush of his beard, a pair of widely spaced gray eyes gazed seriously out at you, faithfully reflecting the changes in humour that the hair on his face otherwise concealed.

He was altogether a new specimen to me, the first of that patchily dressed and unambitious kind I had come into close con-tact with. He asked very little of life except that he should be allowed to go his own way undisturbed amongst his companions, the birds. He had arrived after dark one night, having hitchhiked from Victoria with everything sufficient for his worldly needs car-ried in a cardboard box and a back pack, except for a motorcycle that he had left in Victoria. It seemed that he had lairs, marked by these cardboard boxes containing a few unwanted clothes, in different parts of North America, to which he would return one day, one year, sometime in the future.

On the last day of June, when the cubs were nearly two months old, they discovered a mouse in the downstairs living room. Louis found it behind a chest and chased it, but Louisa caught it and then lost it. Beryl and Stuart took up the chase, the former doubly enthusiastic, not only for the encouragement of her fox cubs, but also because she carries out a relentless war against the mice that invade her house. Stuart eventually caught it and I could tell he was torn between the necessity of encouraging the foxes and saving the mouse, which he would really have preferred to let go. After it was dead, the cubs played with it for a long time, tossing it up in the air and dabbing at it with their paw, just as a cat does, and as the outside foxes always did, but neither cub would eat it.

They celebrated Dominion Day by sharing a box together, for the first time since Louisa had attacked Louis. They became insepar-able and took an enormous amount of exercise. Although our cubs still looked a little smaller than the ones in the run, we were quite sure that they would be the winners if it came to a race. When not sleeping they were so eager to play that Beryl began to worry that they were not getting enough food. But if she fed them one at a time, the one with the food would always leave it to hunt for the other. Louis was death on socks and if a pair for the wash was thrown on the floor he would have one in no time, growling ferociously and working himself into a frenzy of rage. Louisa, looking worried at Louis's excitement, pursued him in a half-hearted way and, if she happened to get hold of the sock, surrendered it without further damage. Outside, she was the more adventurous, already showing the instincts of a hunter.

Their characters were very different. Louisa was the stronger in their games, but she was also shyer and the first to seek her box if strangers arrived. When Beryl crouched on the floor and called to them, they would come up to her with friendly chattering, nibbling at her hair and clothing, but Louis was always the first to arrive and was the more outgoing. Stuart spent a lot of time with them, and they loved to explore the undergrowth of his beard, possibly in the expectation of discovering another mouse there.

During July both the foxes lived downstairs in a kennel similar to the ones outside, and during the day the glass doors of the living room were kept open so that the foxes were free to come and go onto the terrace as they wished. They were particularly active during the night and from upstairs we could hear scurryings and sundry crashes which, in the silence of the night, sounded as if the dresser loaded with crockery had been knocked over. Visitors in the downstairs bedrooms could rarely sleep soundly because of the sniffings and scratchings at their doors. One night a fight developed at four in the morning, and they were discovered tightly wedged between the washing machine and the wall; we were greeted with great delight. Another night a terrible moaning starting downstairs which brought us rushing, hearts beating fast, from our beds. We found that they had switched on the Hoover. They were such mischievous creatures that we had to stop them from venturing upstairs, where there were all sorts of treasures for them to upset or destroy, by fixing a plywood barrier on the stairs.

In their more austere quarters downstairs, no table top was safe from them, although to begin with they could not jump directly onto a table, but reached their objective in a fox child's game of "no feet on the ground," by way of chairs, shelves, and sofas.

The sofas, both downstairs and upstairs, were made from two double beds that we had discovered, when we first arrived, on the site of the old farmhouse known as the "Viny place" and named after the first owners. The farmhouse had long since disappeared, but we discovered the two iron beds, from which both the head and the feet were missing, when investigating some long grass that the cattle had not eaten since they did not like to tread on the bed springs. In this high dry country, the beds were unrusted and in good condition. We slung them from the rafters by ropes and chains. They made comfortable couches, easy to clean underneath and the one downstairs was a constant delight to children who were allowed to swing on it, and to small fox cubs, who found that they could jump onto it.

For the first weeks of July they would not leave the protection of the terrace unless one of us was with them, but even here they had their adventures. Their first awareness of danger came from the peahen who was always after them. Louis narrowly escaped her onslaught by hiding under a chair, where he was found at bay, but she caught Louisa, knocked her down, and struck at her with her feet. Louisa was terrified and for a time afterwards could not straighten her head and neck, a condition caused perhaps more by shock than by actual damage. Although they avoided the peahen until they were larger (and even then took no liberties with her), both soon realized that the peacock was a different kettle of fish, and they loved to stalk his tail as he strutted in front of the house.

Gradually their confidence increased until they ventured as far as the willows, about fifty yards from the terrace. Most of their time outside was spent in play, when they moved as lightly as if on air and seemed hardly to touch the ground as they floated past. They twisted and doubled, and their tails, with the black tip just beginning to show, flicked over their backs as they turned. They were out each morning and evening, but from ten to five during the day they slept inside. The night, still spent in the room downstairs, they passed in play and rest, and in the early morning, when they heard our voices, they called to us from the foot of the stairs.

In preparation for their living outside, we fixed up a large run for them and a kennel adjoining the end of the house. They could get into the run through the kennel door, which could then be closed if we wanted to confine them. The run provided a sanctuary for them from their enemy, the peahen, and they were quick to appreciate this. The day after it was put up, Beryl found the cubs inside and the peahen prowling round the outside, while they watched her, unconcerned and safe. It also provided a sanctuary from the big Afghan nomad dog, Kochi — whom they loved to bait — should she cut off their retreat to the house. In her old age she seemed too stiff to catch them, but that was never a safe assumption.

August was perhaps the best month that we had with the foxes, as they were still completely reliant on us. They used both the outside kennel and the one in the house, sometimes sleeping out and sometimes in.

We started taking them for walks, and they covered ten times the distance we managed, most of the time at their wonderful floating gait, best described as a canter. During these walks they hunted and played, laying ambushes for each other and chasing each other round and round and in and out of the birch scrub. Louisa was the hunter and could catch a vole almost heedlessly, while Louis, content to let her do the hunting, liked to play with it after it was caught. They would swop it around between them. Louis, however, was a great catcher of grasshoppers.

They seemed to get more relaxed and friendly in spite of being out so much. We had not attempted to house train them, thinking them far too nervous for any discipline, but now that they could go outside whenever they wanted they never made a mess in the house, except for rare emotional mishaps when they were greeting us. About this time Beryl saw Louisa grooming herself just like a cat, licking her paw and passing it over her head and ears. Although the cubs in the run and those with us were now almost the same size, the cubs in the run had better coats, probably due to the incessant grooming they were subjected to by the parents. Louisa now seemed to become less nervous and more affectionate, Louis more independent and aggressive. Both loved to share the sofa with Stuart and to be tickled and scratched, but neither of them liked to be picked up. If they came, they came on their own volition and left when they had had enough. It seemed that all was going well and that they were going to stay around the house like dogs as we had hoped.

By October 1, they were living completely outside. Our house was cold, as we kept the door open wide enough for them to come in if they wished. On October 4, in the morning they were not in either kennel. Beryl and I had to go away for the day and did not get back until midnight, when the foxes came in to see us, their feet pattering on the tiles because of the ice on their pads. Next day, in fresh snow, we tracked them all over the sanctuary, searching for their new lying-up place. We discovered where one fox had crossed into a neighbour's field and had then returned; yet we came home none the wiser. A day or two later, Louis was alone in the kennel and when he went off, Stuart followed him hoping that he would be led to Louisa. Louis, happy to have Stuart with him, played about, thinking that this was just another walk. He made several pounces in the snow, but caught nothing and did not go to Louisa.

During the next few days, the snow disappeared and both foxes came regularly to the house. They always appeared before dark, and we supposed that wherever they were spending their day, it was not far away. They were both friendly and unworried. One evening when we were having a dinner party, Louis came up the stairs and ran around the room wagging his tail until Beryl took him down and fed him. She found that Louisa, always shyer with strangers, had also been in and taken two chicks.

On October 14, both foxes came again and, later, when Stuart was putting out the rations for the night, Louisa slipped in and managed to get five chicks in her mouth, which she ran off with. Next evening Louis came by himself and was given half a gopher, the other half being kept for Louisa, but while she was still expected the telephone rang, and a friend told us that her son had found a fox dead on the road, two miles from our house. "A female, the smallest fox that I've ever seen." It was, of course, Louisa. She had been run over.

Louis continued to come nearly every evening. We transferred the run and put it alongside that of the other foxes. We wanted to keep Louis for breeding, since he was unrelated to the other cubs, and we thought that he would be less lonely near the other foxes until we could introduce the other female cub to him. It was easy enough to get him into the run, as he would always follow Beryl or Stuart if they had food for him, but once having tasted freedom he was not prepared to stay in the run and proved to be a veritable Houdini at escaping, for he could climb like a cat. Once he was out he usually stayed away for the following night as if to emphasize his point. The night after that, however, he would be back again, as friendly as ever, and it was obvious that he did not hold his few hours in the lock-up against us.

A two-foot aluminum strip had stopped the other foxes from climbing to the top of the fence, but we had only enough to do three sides of Louis's pen, so that the fence that he shared with the other foxes was without a strip on his side. Louis used this fence, first to get in to the other foxes (from where he was rescued, badly shaken but undamaged, when they attacked him), and later, by an intricate traverse that might have tested the skill of a monkey, to gain the top of the outside fence above the strip of aluminum, thereby escaping again. We decided to leave him until we were certain we could keep him on his own terms. Meanwhile, we had discovered where he was living.

A fresh fall of snow had laid a clean white carpet over the countryside. Stuart and I took the car out to make a tour of the roads and look for fox tracks. We found Louis's tracks on the road two miles away and followed them for a mile until they turned off into the fields, as if heading for home. Stuart followed them and found a maze of tracks, including coyote tracks, round a badger earth in a field half a mile from the house. Then he thought he heard Louis bark a muffled bark which seemed to come from far away, but which, he soon discovered, came from underground. Stuart called him and the little fox appeared from one of the badger holes, showing that he was pleased to see Stuart—he made his welcoming chatter and allowed himself to be rolled over and tickled. He followed Stuart part of the way home and then left him.

Louis paid us two more visits. The first was after we had returned from Calgary with three thousand dead chicks from the hatchery. John, at the hatchery, had said to us on that day, "I sure hate to see these chicks just dumped. It seems such a waste. Now that I know your foxes are getting them, I feel much better about it." After we had arrived home, we had shaken the chicks out of the plastic sacks in which we had collected them and spread them all out on the concrete floor so that they might be quite dry before we divided them into bags of twenty—one day's ration for the foxes—and put them into the deep freeze. While we were doing this, Louis arrived, like a small shadow. His eyes popped at the stupendous sight of so much food, and he darted here and there, trying to collect as many chicks in his mouth as possible, but always dropping one or two as he tried to grab another. Eventually he skipped away and out into the night, his mouth full.

A day or two later, Beryl and Stuart went down to see him in his country house. The snow had gone and the brown fields rolled away under the clear blue sky. Louis came out of the badger earth and allowed Beryl to play with him. Then, with his chittering, he invited her to come into his den; Beryl politely declined. He came a little way back with them and then returned to sit above the earth. He seemed so entirely appropriate there with the country spreading forever around him and the mountains looming in the distance, that Beryl could hardly bring herself to think of shutting him up again; however, he would never find a vixen unless she did so.

He came home for the last time on November 17 and followed Beryl into the pen. We shut the door after him. The next morning he was gone. We immediately set ourselves to fixing the run so that only a ghost fox could escape from it, but he never returned. If we had not wanted him for breeding we would not have tried to shut him up again, and now we felt that in our efforts we had tried him a little too hard; and if we had let him remain in his badger earth, he would still be around.

We never saw him again, but shortly afterwards a friend told us that she had seen a swift fox twenty miles away. She may have been mistaken, although twenty miles would have meant little to Louis. There is no reason why he should not have survived the winter, as we have since had a fox leave us in the late fall and then return in the spring. Perhaps he is still alive, but it seems probable that he would have returned to where he was brought up and where he knew there were other swift foxes for mating. His most likely fate, if he has not been run over, is that he has been killed by some predator: a coyote, a lynx, or a great horned owl.

CHAPTER 5

The Trumpeter Swans

WHEN WE WERE PERSUADED by Clio that having given up sailing we should now try and do something for the endangered wild life in Canada, she also gave us a list of endangered species, which included musk oxen, wood buffalo, black-tailed prairie dogs, the black-footed ferret and trumpeter swans.

Of these, the musk oxen and wood buffalo seemed to be financially inaccessible; the black-footed ferret was so rare that it was not worth considering unless we had a large prairie dog colony; and the prairie dogs themselves, although probably available, would need to be contained within a deep trench filled with cement, or in wire mesh until the colony was safely established. Even then we would not be able to let the dogs roam free — and still remain friends with the neighbouring farmers and ranchers. And we simply hadn't the funds for such elaborate barriers. It was a pleasant idea to have a home on the range where the deer and the antelope played, together with all endangered species, but it was only within the realm of dreams and not compatible either with our finances or our acreage. Since we had about five acres of shallow pond, it seemed that it might be possible for us to do something about trumpeter swans.

The first swans we saw when we came to Alberta were whistlers. A never to be forgotten sight as they flew high towards the North in an irregular V, with one side longer than the other. The lines seemed to undulate across the sky, as one bird followed another in slight adjustments to altitude, and all the time there came to us, land-bound and mud-clotted far below, a joyous yelping tumult of distant sound, like the music of a pack of hounds bursting out of cover on a fresh scent on a still winter's day. Only a dullard could hear it and not be moved, or long to set off, riding the breeze, on some similar adventure. It is the most disturbing sound in Canada, and it can still be heard.

A Natural History of the Birds of Eastern, Central, and North America, by Forbush and May (the most fascinating bird book ever written), tells of the whistlers like this: "To the ornithologist there is no more thrilling sound than the high double or triple note of the leader of a flock of whistling swans and no more thrilling sight than that of the flock, far up in the azure heights, their long necks stretched towards the Pole.... In migration they fly at such immense heights that often the human eye fails to find them, but even then their resonant, discordant trumpetings can be plainly heard. When seen with a glass at that giddy height in the heavens, crossing the sky in their exalted and unswerving flight, sweeping along at a speed exceeding the fastest express train, traversing a continent on the wings of the wind, their long lines glistening silver in the bright sunlight, they present the grandest and most impressive sight in bird life on this continent."

In the fall of 1974, the fourth Trumpeter Swan Society meeting was held at the Delta Wild Fowl Reserve, at the bottom of Lake Manitoba, almost 800 miles west of Calgary. Having arranged for a girl, who had recently obtained her degree in biology, to look after the foxes and to feed the peafowl, and the moose if they turned up, we left home without a care.

Instead of taking the more direct but more heavily travelled Trans-Canada Highway, we chose a parallel route further north, a happy decision since instead of crossing flat prairie, we travelled a road of constant variety. From the buttes and sandy ravines of Drumheller, once the home of dinosaurs, right across to the east, we were with few exceptions in rolling country broken by clumps of aspen and willow, by pools and ponds. The heavy rains, for it had been a wet fall, had kept much of the grain in the ground and had also filled the ponds, so that we saw plenty of duck, all fat and gorged with grain. We drove past the villages of Conquest and Outlook, named as if to relieve the harshness of the countryside, and from time to time, saw the groups of grain elevators that marked the railway. Now that they are painted white or green or blue or a gentle red, they always remind me of children in their best dresses setting off across the fields for a party — giant children from some distant planet, from Mercury perhaps.

It was dark by the time we got to Portage la Prairie at the end of the second day, and next morning we drove out to the Waterfowl Research Station, along a straight embanked road. Presently, reeds and water began to fill the ditches at the side of the road, and soon we were driving through the marsh with glimpses of reed-enclosed pools and channels on either side. Wherever we looked I could see duck on the move and I felt something of the excitement that I had felt in my young days, when I was keen on wildfowling. It reminded me of many rendezvous with duck in many parts of the world. Of cold cramped waits on lonely foreshores in England, of early mornings on the marshes at Tel el Kebir in Egypt, when the water round was alive with ducks and the whirr of wings sounded in the still dark sky above; of the bright colours in India, when the sun already well up, caught the plumage of the birds disturbed at daylight, returning to the jheel; and of the Himalayan snows, in the evening, still alight, when it was too dark to shoot in the plains below. There was always a similarity in the setting; the same or similar birds, the same reeds, and still water where they were resting or wished to rest or feed, in creeks, inlets, pools, and ponds.

The Delta Marsh, between the prairie farmlands and the southern shore of Lake Manitoba, is four miles wide and extends along the shore for about twenty miles. It is separated from the lake by a sandy ridge in which maple, ash, poplar, and willow grow thickly and protect the marsh from the bleak northerly winds. There are several breaks in this ridge, through which the waters of Lake Manitoba ebb and flow according to the wind, and as the lake is over a hundred miles long the ebb and flow can be quite considerable.

The Delta Waterfowl Station began as a hatchery with the object of returning more duck to the marsh than sportsmen took from it. In 1938, the North American Wildlife Foundation took over the Station, and it is now a regular seminary of duck knowledge. The University of Manitoba also has a Field Station a few miles away.

At the meeting of the Trumpeter Swan Society there were so many professors and specialists, most of them American, that Beryl and I felt as if we were the only amateurs, as indeed we were. However, we had already been to one conference and were acquainted with some of the specialists. Knowing that the organizers of such conferences are usually on the lookout for some lecture or film to fill up the time, I had suggested that Beryl and I might show some slides of the foxes and moose in our wildlife reserve. This idea was enthusiastically accepted.

Although we had not yet been promised any swans by the Canadian Wildlife Service, it was a pair of swans we were after. The President of the Trumpeter Swan Society, Ron MacKay, who was also a senior official in the Canadian Wildlife Service, had them in his gift, but probably for fear of creating a precedent had been unwilling to allow private individuals to have them. (In Canada, trumpeters are Royal birds and cannot be owned; they can only be held for the Crown.) Calgary Zoo, however, had too many and were anxious to dispose of them, and everyone at the conference knew that we wanted a pair.

During the three-day conference we were shown several films, all dealing with the American refuges; in all of them there seemed to be a superfluity of four-wheel-drive trucks, motorboats, canoes, outboard engines, and good-looking, active young men — everything necessary (given by the government without stint), to run a wildlife refuge and to catch and band trumpeter swans. In Canada, apart from Ron MacKay, our President, there seemed to be very little help for the same sort of work.

On the last afternoon, I gave my talk and showed slides. In order to provide refuges for nesting, Beryl and I had made four islands on our pond, transporting rocks into the water by dinghy during the summer, and by truck across the ice during the winter. The difficulty in winter was collecting the rocks, which were soon frozen hard into the ground. The first settlers on our place had cleared an immense amount of stones from the fields. These were piled along the field boundaries so that they could be prized loose and loaded into the truck in winter if the truck could get to the pile. When the snow got too deep, Beryl and I used to take a toboggan, roll the stones onto the toboggan, and then pull it to the truck.

One of my slides was a picture of an old man, whom I hated to have to identify as myself, in tattered wind-proof clothing, with a haggard face and gray hair streaming in the wind, together with his wife who is scarcely in better shape, both bowed down as they painfully drag a toboggan loaded with huge rocks over the bleak ice-and-snow-covered steppe. When I explained to the audience that this photo had not been taken in a Siberian gulag; that, in fact, it was Beryl and I on our game farm, hauling stones for the swans' islands, there was a gasp, and at the end of the lecture all the Americans stood up and with one voice cried to Ron MacKay, "Why can't the Smeetons have a pair of trumpeters?" That evening, perhaps against his better judgement, he promised to see what he could do about letting us have a pair. As with the foxes, had Beryl and I known the expense and the work that a pair of swans were going to involve us in, we might have opted instead for a short term in a prison camp.

When we got home we started to think about a place in which we could keep them until the pond was no longer frozen. Since our swans almost certainly would be pinioned birds, they would not be able to escape from lynx and coyote on the frozen pond. We knew that lynx came into the reserve after the rabbits; we had lost two peafowl and one snowy owl to lynx. If a lynx can get its head through a hole, the rest of its body can follow like quicksilver, and I'd often seen their tracks in the snow, showing that they went through the six-inch wire mesh of the fence with barely a pause. On rare occasions we had spotted coyotes within the reserve, but since we had taken great trouble to fill all the gaps with field stones where the bottom of the fence was a little high, we assumed they squeezed through a hole under the gate in the southeast corner. Although a log stopped the hole, we didn't always remember to replace it when the gate was in use. (Our assumption turned out to be wrong. Kochi, not the log, kept the coyotes away. Only since she's retired and become an old-age pensioner have we seen them regularly.)

In preparation for the day when our trumpeters might arrive, we went to see Archie Hogg, an ardent lover of all wildfowl, at his ranch south of Okotoks. The ranch lies at the end of a gravel road, in rolling grassland country which sweeps grandly up towards the Rockies, not many miles away. We asked our way at an isolated farmhouse belonging to a farmer, also called Hogg. "Just go right on to the end of the road," he told us. "You'll find nothing but Hoggs 'round here."

Archie Hogg had started with a wounded trumpeter that had been brought to him and ever since he had had one or two trumpeters, together with whistlers and Canada geese, on the pool just below his house. Some are free-flying wild birds, some have their wings clipped, and some, like the trumpeters, are pinioned.

His pond was smaller than ours, and surrounded by reeds — a secret place, encompassed by the rolling prairie of the foothills and the mountains beyond. It had proved too small for both breeds of swan to live in harmony, and six Whistlers had been killed by trumpeters. We asked him what he did with them in the winter.

"Well, those that stay, I just put in there," he replied, pointing to a shed surrounded by a small enclosure.

"Do you keep them in there all the winter?"

"Fine days they come out, but mostly they stay inside. I shut them up at night."

"Do you give them any heat, like a brooder lamp or anything?"

"No," he said, "I just give them plenty of straw."

"Do you clean the shed out from time to time?" we asked.

"No. Their droppings build up and it keeps them warm."

At Delta the importance of keeping the swans' quarters clean had been stressed lest they should develop enteritis or some such disease, but Archie Hogg had his own ideas and they seemed to work.

I asked him if birds from Grande Prairie came to his pond. He said that they passed over on their migration, but he doubted if they would stop at the pond, since his own birds were there and they were very aggressive about their territory.

"One day," he told us, "on a foggy morning, I was out not far from here when I heard a trumpeter calling, the call getting louder so I knew he was coming towards me. Presently two birds appeared flying low over a wire fence, coming out of the midst and flying close past me. As they flew they kept calling and looking behind them, and soon a third bird appeared, a cygnet, struggling along and trying to keep up with the older birds. It was interesting to see how they were worried about it and trying to encourage it. But they didn't stop. Tired as the young swan was, they avoided my pond."

Our second contact was Mrs. Lesowski, who lived near Lumby, east of Vernon. When we found the house, a stalwart middle-aged man was doing something to a truck outside. On learning his name, I asked if it was his wife who looked after trumpeters. "No," he said, "It's my mother. She's inside. Go right in."

A small and elderly, but extremely vigorous woman, with astonishing black hair, met us at the door. She took us into a kitchen and living room where everything was rubbed so clean, Beryl and I

Taffy on the roof of his den.

After stretching and pausing for a scratch, Harold is all set for the day.

Louis at his country house.

TOP *Mrs. Newcombe.*
BOTTOM *Louis emerges from the badger hole that he had adopted.*

Louisa at the telephone.

Harriet, Mrs. Newcombe's daughter.

Peterkin.

Stepping proudly.

TOP *Pollux, Petruska and Hardy.*
BOTTOM *Peterkin tolerates his calves as they push in under his horns at feeding time.*

TOP *Beryl with one-year-old Petruska, her favourite.*
BOTTOM *Castor and Pollux with their first horns and author.*

Mary as a calf.

TOP *Beryl with Martha and Mary.*
BOTTOM *George Kollin, "Bison George," at his studies.*

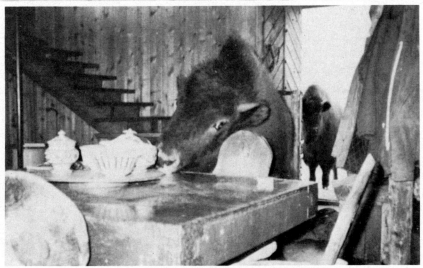

TOP *The bison in front of the house.*
BOTTOM *Mary sneaks inside to eat the butter.*

The author and Mary.

TOP *The upstairs living room.*
BOTTOM *The glass doors that Peterkin liked to tap.*

The author and Kochi.

felt like two bears who had wandered in leaving muddy footmarks on the oilcloth of the porch.

After giving us coffee and cookies, she settled back in her chair in the manner of one well used to being interviewed by the press, or by "those people," as she described the scientists of the Fish and Wildlife Service with whom she was so often in contact.

"So you want to know something about trumpeters," she started. "Though I say it myself, you've come to the right place. Those people never tell you anything that makes sense. The first trumpeter I had was a young bird that was brought to me. I guess he wasn't ready to fly. I had him for seven years. I called him Marcus."

"Where did you keep him?" I asked.

"In summer he was on the pond, and in winter he came to the house. We have a good pond, but of course, it is all frozen in winter. He used to live under the verandah there."

The windows of a room that formed part of the basement of the house looked under the verandah. The verandah had been boarded up on the outside, and it made a roomy shelter for swans. Mrs. Lesowski explained that it was a very convenient arrangement because they could be fed and have their water changed by opening a basement window. She now had two birds that the Wildlife Service had given her to look after.

"They can look through the window into the house. They like it. It makes them feel right at home," she explained. "But that Marcus! He often came right into the house anyway. He was always around when I was cooking, asking for treats. That was a nuisance sometimes. His head was higher than the table and he liked to help himself."

"Didn't he need to get into water at times?" Beryl wanted to know.

"Oh yes," she replied. "Every Saturday I used to put him in the bath. I'd run the water, then pick him up. He never struggled. Then I'd put him in the bath and shut the door. 'You let me know when you want to come out,' I'd say to him, and sure enough, after about an hour, he'd start calling me."

"When he was on the pond," Beryl asked, "how did you stop him from flying away?"

"I used to keep one wing clipped. No problem. I used to say, 'Show me your wings, Marcus.' He'd hold them out and I'd cut the flight feathers on one wing."

"Was he ever sick?"

"Oh yes. They get sick sometimes. Off their feed, or diarrhea. Then I give them some medicine."

"What sort of medicine?" This was just the kind of information Beryl was after.

"Pink medicine."

"But do you know what kind?"

"It was just medicine. I get it from the drugstore. I'll show you the bottle. I ask for Marcus's medicine now." She brought out the bottle which had no label and was filled partly with fluid and partly with a pink sediment. "That soon fixes them," she said. Our minds boggled as we thought of the biologists with Ph.D.'s who came to talk with her.

"It was too bad that those people had to take Marcus away," she told us again as we said good-bye. "They won't look after him properly. However, they've given me two birds. They are on the pond now but we'll bring them in soon. They'll never be like Marcus, though. He was my baby."

After these visits it was obvious to us that, although the swans would be all right in summer on the pond without a house, in winter the swans would need a shelter and a small enclosure as near to the house as possible. We did not think that we could ever hope to get on the same terms with them as Mrs. Lesowski had with Marcus, but we hoped to do as well as Archie Hogg. We decided to put up a small enclosure at the corner of the drive fence where it turned to join the house, fifty yards away, and to build an octagonal house, similar to the peafowls' house. Being the second of its kind, the house was a better job, with double walls, plywood inside and old eight-inch shiplap outside, and a green asbestos tile roof. It was the most delightful and regal home for Royal birds; a gazebo, with a view down to the pond and to the mountains beyond. It was joined to the angle of the drive fence by snow fencing.

Stuart had now been with us some months. He never went outside without his binoculars, and consequently he had identified a number of birds that, up to then, I had missed. He was good with his hands and very meticulous in all he did, except in the way he dressed. Another young bird watcher, Jamey Podlubny, had found his way to our place and often used to come to see us. Unlike Stuart, he was always neatly dressed in clothes suitable for the climate and for what he was doing—watching birds. He did this every weekend, hitch-hiking out of Calgary, wearing a green Austrian hat with an owl's feather stuck in the band, and carrying a small pack with a sleeping bag and food. Although not yet twenty, he was extraordinarily self-sufficient. He was quite prepared to spend the night in a snowbank if darkness overtook him in some of the wilder places that he frequented, nor did he think it a special hardship if he had to sleep out in a pup tent when the thermometer was well below zero. He was always ready to help with any project that was going on and was almost embarrassingly careful not to be a nuisance. We rarely got him to stay for a meal. To mention a meal was almost to ensure that he would say that he had just eaten, or that he had some food in his pack and had to be on his way. He and Stuart got on extremely well together, although there was considerable difference in age, and on the few occasions when Jamey stayed the night, they would stay up talking until the small hours of the morning. From our bedrooms, we would hear their voices, sounding like the contented chatter of duck on a pond.

Jamey and Stuart gave us a hand with the swan's house. Stuart laid the roof tiles with particular care. But nothing took precedence over their interest in birds, and suddenly, at the sight of a distant bird, or the sound of a "cheep" passing overhead, all work would stop, ladders and tools would fly to the ground, and a mad rush would be made for binoculars.

Stuart had not been with us very long before Beryl gave him his first job. She had bought two or three great earthenware jars, in which the Chinese used to ship their pickled eggs. She wanted a wooden lid cut out of plywood to fit over the top. "Now you can make me a collage to go on the lid," she told Stuart, giving him some programs from the Exhibition of Chinese Art that had been touring Canada, from an exhibition of Inuit art, and various other coloured magazines. Stuart was soon surrounded by cutouts and coloured bits of paper, squatting barefoot on the floor, frowning seriously as he moved his cutouts into different places on the lid and then reviewed them from different angles.

For three days, Stuart was totally lost in his collage.

"He'll never finish," I told Beryl, "and anyway I don't think he's got a clue as to what he's doing."

In the end, after all the cuttings had been stuck down and treated with three coats of varnish, I had to admit that he had made a very artistic job. Waxwings, pintail, redpolls, and squirrels were mixed with reproductions of Chinese art treasures, and an Inuit painting of musk oxen galloping across the snow, cut to represent the steam coming out of a jade teapot. All the colours were most skillfully blended.

In spite of such interruptions, we were more or less ready by the time we heard from the zoo in October that they had two swans for us — a male and a female (or a "cob" and a "pen," as they are properly called). The pen was two years older than the male, who was three. When we went to collect them in our truck, the keeper had no trouble catching the pen, but for the cob he had to use a landing net in which the swan became quite entangled and never thereafter forgot his alarming experience. We stuffed the birds each into a sack, and they lay quietly as we drove back to the house. It took them about three days to settle down in their new home, during which period they spent most of their time looking for a way to get out. We were also busy raising the height of the enclosure and wiring it up more efficiently to prevent a lynx getting at them, by adding a roof of wire netting, so that they had plenty of time to get used to us.

We fed them wheat, bread, and lettuce, all of which they liked to dabble in their water before eating. I enjoyed watching the bread gradually work its way down their long white necks. They never used the house as a shelter and would only just go into the entrance if we put their feed and water inside. No matter what the weather, nor how bitter the wind, they preferred to be outside, squatting facing the wind, their heads under their wings. They were always very alert, and any movement outside the house would at once be noticed. Their heads would then come out from under their wings, their long necks straight up and down, as they investigated for the cause of the noise or examined the movement.

The pen, who we had named Leda, was the larger and dominant bird and would not allow the cob, Zeus, to take bread or food before her. They became much tamer but were always suspicious of any untoward movement, which they greeted with a note of alarm, a short "kek" repeated at intervals. In order to provide them with a place to swim, we put an old dinghy in the enclosure and filled it with water. Unfortunately, freezing weather soon arrived and turned the pool into an ice rink. As the winter wore on the swans began to look rather scruffy so we put a water heater in the dinghy, used for keeping a cattle watering trough open, and from then on they always had somewhere to bathe, something which they did every day.

It was a bitterly cold January; yet they made no use of their house. In order to give them shelter, we made a wall of hay bales within the enclosure, and Zeus used to sit close to the hay bales. Leda had discovered that the wood of the dinghy was warm from the heated water within and used to snuggle up to it. By late February, they appeared to have reversed roles. Zeus was now the more aggressive. He would grab at Stuart's fingers or at his coat, and once gave him a buffet with his wing. Leda became more gentle.

They first trumpeted in the middle of March, when a plane flew low over the house, and from then on they always stood up, beat their wings, and trumpeted to any low-flying aircraft. They gave a short call to Stuart every morning when he went to feed them. Zeus would then make a show of aggression, hissing and advancing towards Stuart, snapping at his fingers and then escorting him to the gate when he left, but we thought that his welcoming trumpet made up for any subsequent hostility. In fact both birds were avid welcomers. If we had been out in the car, they greeted our return with tremendous trumpeting and wing flapping.

One morning in early April I noticed that the snow in the enclosure was spotted in places with small purple stains, which I thought might be traces of blood in the snow, and Leda was off her feed. In fact she took no feed but drank a lot. Next morning she was obviously very sick. I watched her from the window as she huddled up to the dinghy dipping her beak disconsolately into the water. And as I was watching her, she keeled over and died.

I took her body out of the enclosure, and Zeus blamed me for stealing her away. His manner towards me changed, and for a long time he was suspicious if I came near.

We took Leda to Edmonton for a post mortem. She had died from a particularly violent enteritis, and we were comforted to a certain extent by hearing that we could not have done anything to save her, that there was no reason to suspect that Zeus would have picked up the bug, and that she might have been infected before she came to us and had succumbed to the illness because of stress. Stress is inevitable with captive birds, especially with those confined at the time of mating and migration, and the condition must be even worse for pinioned birds. We decided that if we were given a mate for Zeus we would not confine the swans again.

A few days after the death of Leda, one end of the pond thawed. We opened the gate to Zeus's enclosure and the gates leading into the game park. It took Zeus some time to decide on his move, but he knew exactly where he was going. Towards evening he set out for the small shallow slough just below the house. There he stayed until dusk, ducking his head into the water and splashing it over his back, but it was shallow enough for a coyote to get him if one happened to be in the reserve. By the time Beryl and I had had supper, he was in a marshy patch a little nearer to the pond.

"We'll have to drive him into the pond," said Beryl, "I'll never sleep until I know he's safe."

We put on our boots and went down towards him, talking to him so that he should not be alarmed. We could see his tall white shape moving slowly ahead of us through the dead grass and scrub, still untouched by the fingers of spring, and from time to time we heard his faint distrustful "kek." He was taking things easily; and from time to time, he squatted down to rest. At last he reached the edge of the pond where he launched himself into the water and we heard the "waters wap and the waves wan" as he paddled out — a dim white shape under the stars.

C H A P T E R   6

More About Moose

In THE SPRING OF THE YEAR that the swans came to us, we had three
moose in the game park; Petruska and her twin sons, Castor and
Pollux. Petruska had not shown us her first calf for over a
month. With the twin bulls she took three weeks before she
brought them to the house, although she had come up to Beryl a
week before and thereafter Beryl had fed her from a bucket in the
woods, seeing the calves lurking shyly close behind, or knowing
that they were hidden near. We were interested to see what she
would do this year.

On May 10, the young bulls came alone to the house. They were
both nervous and kept looking towards the west. It was the first
time that they had been to the house by themselves, and Beryl felt
sure that Petruska had driven them away and had either calved or
was about to calve. We still believed that it was better to allow
Petruska to do things by herself, as she wanted to, rather than to go
out and look for her. Ten days later when we still had not seen her,
two friends arrived for lunch.

"I see that Petruska has two lovely chestnut calves," said one,
more used to describing horses than moose.

"Oh," cried Beryl, "How marvellous." She was much relieved as
she is always anxious at this time. Then, like any grandmother, she
asked, "What are they?"

"We weren't close enough to tell," she replied. "She was by
the fence, and mother and children looked as if they were doing
very well."

Next day, Petruska brought her calves to the house, but found
on her arrival that her sons were already waiting at the door. She
immediately put back her ears and charged them, and the bulls took

45

off in an instant, one to the south and the other to the east. No sooner had Petruska seen Castor on his way than she wheeled round and set off after Pollux, who had not run far since he was in no immediate danger. Pollux sprinted across the marshy slough just below the house, with Petruska splashing close behind, followed by her two long-legged and very confused calves looking like two golden retrievers at her heels. Her sons were well grown and swift, so Petruska did not press her pursuit, but returned instead to the house, bringing her new calves with her. We were soon able to see from the narrow, light-coloured triangles under their tails that they were both cows.

"Clever Petruska," Beryl cooed. "You're so clever, aren't you? First a girl, then two boys and now two girls."

Petruska thrust out her smooth brown nose as she begged for bread. She was in a proper mess. Her coat was only half shed, so that she looked bare in patches, and there were long scratches where twigs had pulled out the winter coat as she brushed through the trees. From her mane a soft roll of under-hair hung down her neck like a frayed collar and, after her five calves in three years, she was looking thinner than ever before. Yet, now that the leaves were out in that marvellous month when the country seems to step straight into summer, we knew that she would soon be sleek and smooth again.

About this time, first Castor and then, a few days later, Pollux got a fetlock full of porcupine quills. We never know whether the moose run into the porcupines by mistake, or whether they cannot resist striking at them when they see them. Probably they strike at them because it always seems to happen when the moose are young. The quills gradually dropped out and ultimately they suffered no lasting ill effects although the lameness and swelling lasted for some weeks.

Petruska's condition steadily improved, and in the beginning of August she was already trying to wean the calves. She moaned and broke away if they attempted to suck; nevertheless, they usually managed to get a mouthful on the move. "The Girls," as they came to be called, were also very keen on making the acquaintance of the two bulls, much to their mother's dismay. What with weaning the calves and keeping Castor and Pollux away, Petruska was kept pretty busy.

At the end of August, both bulls rubbed the velvet off their horns, and from then on all the moose began to move about together as a herd. We saw Castor and Pollux having serious trials of strength. Although Castor was the more aggressive, he was handicapped by an injured horn, which had not grown since he'd damaged it in the spring and which finally broke off short during one of his tussles with Pollux.

One day when Pollux was standing outside the house, gazing to the south, I passed close to him on my way down to the pond. I suddenly heard the rush of hooves behind me and turned round to find Pollux in pursuit. He had always been the gentler of the bulls, however at the time of the rut moose are not predictable. I had a stick with which to wallop him, but it was probably my voice, loud, indignant, and perhaps alarmed that stopped him. He ran away, bleating. He was still very young.

When, halfway through September, Petruska first came in estrus and turned on her charm and her various wiles to tempt her sons, Beryl and I thought that neither bull appeared to know what it was all about. But when she came on again, three weeks later, Pollux seemed to have been reading up on the situation. He chased Castor into temporary exile and bred Petruska successfully after going through the customary preliminary courting procedures — resting his chin on her quarters and performing flehmen (nuzzling her genitals, raising his head, and curling his lips as if in disdain). Petruska, for her part, issued long plaintive bleats at his approach and then coyly rushed away from him, always stopping before he might think that she had really gone. The actual consummation of all this love-making lasted only a few seconds and seemed to be rather an inadequate reward for such a long period of mooning and yearning. Before the end of October, Castor was back with the herd.

November was Petruska's best month. She had shaken off the responsibilities that she felt for her calves and she was not yet feeling the effects of the embryo that she was carrying. Occasionally, if something such as a distant view of our neighbour, Mr. Fox, riding his horse as he checked his cows, had excited her, we might see her running with her mane up, striking at bushes as she had done when she was a calf.

On a fine morning towards the middle of the month, Beryl set off with Stuart to burn up some piles of trees that had been pushed down by a bulldozer in an attempt to clear some ground, before we bought the place. As they moved through the woods, they came upon the five moose browsing in a scattered group. Petruska moved to meet Beryl, and then, seeing Stuart, put on her "bonnet face" — Beryl's description of her when she pins her ears down — and advanced on him. Stuart moved quickly behind some young poplars, but Petruska reared up and struck at him. It was more a gesture than an attack, but Stuart looked round for better cover.

"It's all right, Stuart," Beryl called. "I'll go on, and she'll follow me."

Off she went in her old wind-proof jacket, matches in her pocket and a can of oil in her hand, and as she walked she called "Petrooska, Petrooska," her voice fading into the trees. Petruska paid absolutely no attention. Her mind was on other things.

Beryl reached the woodpile and, in the interest of starting the fire, forgot all about Stuart's plight. When at last a good blaze was going, she thought that she had better go and find what was keeping him and walked back taking approximately the same route that she had come. As she picked her way back through the trees, she saw a large brown object, high up in an aspen. For a moment she thought it was a bear, but when she got nearer she discovered it was Stuart, wedged in the fork of an aspen, his legs drawn up and his beard shrouding his knees. There was no need to ask what he was doing; Petruska was patrolling beneath the tree.

This time Petruska followed Beryl and the siege of Stuart was relieved. Stuart had always had a great respect for Petruska, ever since he had seen her strike at me when I had had the temerity to examine a wart on her stomach. Now his respect was enhanced.

"You left me," he called reproachfully after Beryl. "She'd have had me if I hadn't climbed this tree." From then on, Stuart's affection for the moose diminished.

Even if we supplied them with a little supplementary feeding, it was obvious we could not keep five moose in 160 acres. The maximum number of moose the reserve can sustain is two, together with their calf or calves, until it is time for the new calf to be born. Doctor Val Geist of Calgary University, a specialist in ungulates and a man of youthful enthusiasms, advised us to keep the two bull calves, if the place could stand it.

"They have to get rid of their aggressive tendencies," he told us, "and if they're kept together, they'll work those tendencies out on each other, rather than on you. I had my doubts about Peterkin, you know. A bottle-fed moose never has the right respect for humans. As he got older you might have found him a bit of a menace."

One day Val came to see us and brought his children. We packed into the Landrover and drove round looking for the moose. Where we found them browsing, the trees and bushes were in full leaf and they were difficult to see, so we got out of the car and moved closer for a better look. As soon as Petruska saw Beryl she came pushing through the bushes towards us. Val and the children and I moved back a little towards the car, a precautionary move, as we never know how Petruska will react to strangers, when away from the house. Beryl went forward to meet her, and the moose, with ears pricked, came up to her and nuzzled her, begging for bread.

"Look at that," Val said to his children, "Anyone can see that that moose loves Beryl. But then," he added after brief reflection, "Beryl is the only moose mother who has never rejected her child."

We decided to follow Val's advice about the bulls, but we were now faced with the problem of disposing of The Girls. We did not want to sell them to a zoo, where they would find the area limited, after the freedom that they had enjoyed in the game park. Nor were we happy about turning them loose, after they had been living for a year in a protected environment. We had, however, been asked by the Director of Northwest Trek, a game park near Tacoma, if we could let them have a calf. As we had already been there, we knew it was a big park, which visitors drove through in a park-transport system. It only keeps animals indigenous to North America and is a place of hills, woods, meadows, and streams, with the secrecy and space that a moose needs. We agreed to send one of the twins there in the spring when Petruska would be driving them away anyway.

Soon after arranging this, we had a telephone call from Wisconsin from a Mr. Johnson, a man with a vigorous and persuasive voice. He had a hundred acres of aspen, spruce, and marsh, in which he wanted to put some moose, and he understood we might have a calf to dispose of. He told us that he was not going into the moose-meat business, that he would be glad to take our calf, and that we might be sure that it would be well looked after. He kept telephoning at monthly intervals to find out how the calves were doing, and he forwarded a cheque in down payment.

We had entered the moose business more or less unintentionally and now realized we had an opportunity of getting something back on our expenses. Moose are rarely found in captivity, as full-grown moose are difficult to capture or to handle without loss when captured. Abandoned calves have been found difficult to raise, consequently, moose calves, particularly yearlings, fetch a good price. Nevertheless, we decided to make a firm rule that we would never let a calf go to anything less than an enclosure of forty acres, and to exact a guarantee from the purchaser that the animal would not be sold again.

In September of that year, the Calgary Zoo asked us if we would take an abandoned calf that had been brought to them. It had been living in an out station, which the zoo had established to receive neglected or injured animals that are brought to them from time to time, but they were having difficulty giving it adequate care. The calf was taking milk from a bucket and was also destined, if it survived, for Northwest Trek. We said that we would look after it until the two moose were ready to be shipped in the spring.

Next day the zoo truck arrived and a bull calf was turned loose in the drive. He had been in a small enclosure and had been looked after by college students as holiday work so that he was very tame, but was only half the size of Petruska's twins, born at the same time. He was a really seedy little moose, with a bad coat. Beryl immediately put him on a much increased ration of canned milk and milk replacer, a powder which is mixed with water and is common in the cattle business. He was never satisfied. The zoo had said they would give us a dollar a day for his keep, but "Oliver," as he was inevitably called, drank eight cans of evaporated milk in one day.

Beryl telephoned the zoo to say she could not afford to keep him at that rate. Neither could they, the zoo replied. A compromise was arrived at and the zoo sent us some cases of canned milk and sacks of milk replacer. Oliver soon waxed fat and grew wonderfully, but he remained far behind the twins. We kept him in the drive, as we did not know what sort of a reception he would be given by the other moose. He used to come to the door of the house for his milk. Since this is a stable type door, the bucket could be hooked on the top of the lower half. Oliver, in his enthusiasm, would splash milk all over the door and over the stone step beneath, where it then set hard and could not be removed without a great deal of scrubbing.

Eventually the day came when we had to separate Petruska from her calves. We opened the gate leading to the drive and Petruska, always ready to explore new ground, led her calves through. Beryl enticed her back inside with some bread and shut the gate before the calves followed. They did not seem to be unduly worried as they had themselves and Oliver, whom they quickly discovered, for company. The family ties weren't completely severed, however, for all the moose rested together, Petruska and the two bulls on one side of the fence, The Girls and Oliver on the other.

Before sending Petruska's first calf (the only calf we ever sold to a zoo) to Calgary, we had trained her to enter the zoo's trailer for her feed, but when moving day came and we shut the door on her, she became very alarmed, and during the short journey was under considerable stress. It took her a long time to settle down in her new home, and although she had a good area, spent most of the time hidden in a shed. She was off her feed and miserable. Beryl, who was almost in the same condition, went to sit with her, although whether this did either of them any good was questionable.

In order to avoid this stress, our local vet, John Quine (who is always ready to give advice or pay the animals a visit but never to send a bill) suggested that, when next we were shipping calves, we should try Atravet, a tranquilizing drug which can be administered in small doses over long periods with no ill effects, and which is easily given in a slice of banana—a fruit all moose seem to enjoy. As it was difficult to differentiate between The Girls, and as both were greedy, both were given Atravet. We borrowed the trailer from the zoo and soon the moose were going in readily for their feed.

In April the truck arrived from Northwest Trek, with two travelling boxes which looked as if they would barely contain the bigger calf. We decided to lure whichever of The Girls came first into the zoo trailer, and to load her from there to a travelling box. Two young men had arrived from the zoo to help with the loading and together with Stuart and the truck drivers we had a crew of five. This army was concealed so that the calves would not be disturbed while Stuart crouched behind the tree, near the back of the trailer, like a primitive man in ambush. As soon as the first calf went in, he leapt to the door and slammed it shut. It was then that the effect of Atravet became obvious. Instead of behaving as if she were in a trap, the calf remained quite undisturbed, but she was reluctant to go forward into the travelling box. We jacked up the rear end of the trailer and I went inside and pushed her from behind. Slowly, but with equanimity, she slid forwards into the box and the drop door was let down.

Oliver was such a tame little moose that there was no need to put him into the trailer first. He looked mildly into his travelling box, and before he knew what had happened was hustled inside. Both boxes were then loaded into the truck and lashed down. Oliver took the opportunity of a brief wait, before they started on their long journey, to lie down.

Stuart was leaving us for a time and was delighted to get a free lift to Tacoma. He took with him a bunch of bananas, and some moose buns that Beryl had made of powdered milk, honey calf-starter pellets and Atravet. We knew that the moose would be well looked after on the road, and since Stuart was fond of health foods and economically minded, I would not have been surprised if he had eaten one of the buns himself.

When they left, Oliver was again on his feet, and both moose looked quietly out of their boxes, like ponies on their way to a pony-club meet. I think Beryl and I were more upset than they were. Stuart wrote to say that they had arrived safely, but that both moose had been shaky on their legs when they got out. We have found that they travel best in a large box where they have room to move about and to lie down if they wish, rather than a small box where, with the exception of a small moose like Oliver, there is no room for them to get down. In a large box they soon get their balance and are not thrown about.

The remaining twin, now known as "Girlie," was turned out again with the other moose and she was over a year old when Mr. Johnson arrived from Wisconsin with his daughter, Nikki, and a large trailer. Mr. Johnson, as we had expected from his voice on the telephone, turned out to be a large and confident man, and Nikki a tall and extremely good-looking fair girl, who was going to be the moose farmer. Beryl could not have chosen a better person for the remaining twin to go to. Mr. Johnson could not be restrained from offering advice about the boxing in a loud voice, which upset the moose. He was persuaded to return to the house where Nikki pushed him into a bedroom from where he could watch, but not interfere with the loading. They drove non-stop to Wisconsin and with typical kindness rang up immediately to say that the moose had travelled well.

Mr. Johnson had brought us a small cast iron moose as a gift, a fitting termination for the rail at the top of the stairs, which Beryl had made out of the iron teeth of an old-fashioned horse hay rake.

Any old bit of iron is an irresistible attraction to Beryl, which, once found, will be hung onto for years, until some use for it is discovered. The low winter sun casts the shadow of the iron moose onto the wall behind the stairs, so that we involuntarily glance at the window to see if the real moose are there.

News of "The Girls" is good. Both have flourished, but Oliver, gentle, friendly Oliver, was found dead in his large demesne, apparently killed by an older bull.

When we had taken the dead swan for a post mortem in Edmonton, we had met Barry Gilbert of the Fish and Wildlife Service, who had an office at the top of the same building. He was interested in the formation of an experimental game farm, for the study of indigenous wild animal behaviour under domestic conditions, with a view to game farming on a large scale in areas where forest, muskeg, and black fly prohibit economical cattle raising. For this purpose he wanted animals that could be easily handled. He had heard about Beryl's success with her moose, and now asked if he could have the next offspring. Barry was young, vigorous, and enthusiastic, as yet apparently shackled by no bureaucratic chains. His office had the appearance of a temporary resting place, where he had thrown down his coat for a moment.

"My idea," he told us, "is that if calves are handled at birth, they will then have no fear of humans. I'd like to try this out, and if you could let me know when the moose is going to calve, I'll come right over."

"She might let me handle them," Beryl said, unwilling that anyone should attempt to usurp her special relation with Petruska. "She has never shown any anxiety at my approaching them. It's only the calves that have been nervous. I don't mind having a try, but I'm quite sure that she would never let you get near them."

"Perhaps you are right," Barry admitted reluctantly, "still, I'd like to come over as soon as you think that she's ready to calve."

"The difficulty is to know when," said Beryl, "but if we put her in the drive we ought to be able to keep an eye on her easily enough."

We put Petruska in the drive, and on May 16 she was restless and obviously about to calve. She would take no food and in the afternoon was pacing up and down the drive fence, with her tail up. Beryl telephoned Barry and told him that she thought Petruska was ready to calve any moment and that she had got her tail up.

"Is all of it up?" asked Barry.

"Yes," Beryl told him, "all three inches."

When Barry arrived that evening he said, "I've been thinking about that silly question about her tail. I must have been thinking about cattle. I said to my wife, "I bet I haven't heard the last of it.""

Beryl went up to the end of the drive and found that Petruska had given birth to twins in a secluded place, well hidden from the drive and the road, under a spruce tree. We all went to see her after dinner, Beryl on the inside and Barry and I on the outside of the drive fence. Petruska had two healthy calves, chocolate in colour. Next morning they had dried to a light chestnut. From the other side of the fence we could see that the calves were a bull and a cow. On the inside of the fence Beryl went up to Petruska who came a few steps to meet her and take food from the bucket. The cow calf then came up and Beryl was able to touch it. Petruska left the cow calf with Beryl and went back to the bull. Beryl approached Petruska several times on that day, and on one or two occasions Petruska put her ears back in mild protest.

In the afternoon, thinking that there was not enough feed where the calves were lying, we cut some willow, which we tied in bundles. Beryl started to bind these bundles to the aspen trunks where Petruska was resting, thinking that she would be more inclined to pull them from the tree than if the twigs were lying on the ground. While Beryl was doing this, Petruska made a short charge, but stopped when she put her arms down and spoke to her. The cow calf came up several times and sucked Beryl's finger, which she had dipped in milk, but the bull calf kept away.

Barry went up in the afternoon, still on the other side of the fence, in order to take some photographs. Petruska objected to this and charged right up to the fence. "She looked so mean," he said, "that I couldn't help stepping back and getting behind a tree, although I knew quite well that she couldn't get me."

The next few days were cold and windy. We found that Petruska had left the calves and had been at the willow patch during the night. She had also come down to the house. I felled some aspen and left them lying so that she could get at the top leaves. Meanwhile, Beryl had made progress with the calves and was petting the female, which she had named "Bossie." The male, called "Greedy," because he was always after his mother's teats, was slower in coming to hand, but he too was now sucking Beryl's finger and allowing her to pet him.

We had friends coming to dinner, and on their arrival they told us that they had just been petting our moose calves.

"You mean you touched them?"

"Yes. We got out to take a photograph and they came right up to us."

"Did you see the cow?"

"Yes. She was grazing not far away and didn't seem at all bothered."

They were ranch people and would have recognized any sign of danger, but Beryl and I, who knew how mean Petruska could be, winced at the thought. They were probably near enough to their car to get away if she had turned nasty. As so often happens, when no danger is expected, none occurs. If I had touched the calves then, I believe she would put on a demonstration, sensing my wariness. A few days later, when we had turned them into the game park, I was able to go right up to them; however, Beryl was distracting Petruska with a bucket of feed, which is usually Petruska's primary interest.

That year Castor had a better rack than Pollux and easily dominated the gentler bull. As a result, it was he that bred Petruska in September and Pollux who was driven into temporary solitude. Owing to Peterkin having been a moose from a different part of the country from where Petruska had been found, we were not worried about this inbreeding. However, we did not intend to allow it to go any further. Castor remained a mean moose and, some time before Petruska calved, he gave her a vicious prod in order to drive her away from the feed bowl.

"You devil," Beryl cried, siezing a stick and rushing to the aid of her beloved. "If you do that again, Castor, I'll sell you."

Castor seemed to take this threat so much to heart that a few days later he jumped out over the fence, only bending down the top two feet of the seven-foot fence. He was seen that afternoon in a neighbouring field, and next day at a cattle water trough, and as far as we know has not been seen again. We get constant reports of moose being in the vicinity and inquiries as to whether ours are missing. One of these may have been Castor. There seem to be more moose about and we wonder whether ours attract them. With luck, Castor is still at large, breeding fine moose, and enjoying his freedom.

Sometime in the late fall, when Bossie and Greedy were well-grown calves and before Castor's escape, Barry Gilbert telephoned to ask if he could come over with an assistant to test out a radio tracking collar on a moose calf. It was a very sophisticated collar which would give an indication of the moose's activities: resting, feeding, being placid or alarmed. They wished to compare the signals from the collar with what the moose was actually doing, so that they might learn to interpret the "beeps" on their receiver correctly.

Petruska, Bossie, and Greedy used to come into the drive every day in order to have their feed. Otherwise Castor and Pollux, who had shed their velvet and now had their second-year horns, would drive them away from the feed bowls. It was, therefore, easy to keep Bossie and Greedy in the drive until Barry and his assistant arrived. While the two calves were given another feed, Barry tried the collar on Greedy, who was now the easiest to handle of the two. It was too small for our calves. Barry made an extension to the collar from some copper that we had in the workshop, but by the time that it was finished, it was too late to do anything more that night. Next morning it was again fitted on Greedy who accepted it without any trouble and seemed unaware that it was there. Barry's assistant, Don, put up an aerial like a TV aerial on his pack-radio set, and presently the moose wandered away. Don said that he was getting excellent reception.

At about noon, he thought that the moose must be resting, since there was no sign of movement and the beep was very steady. At about three o'clock, Don was getting rather restive.

"There is absolutely no change in their position," he said. "It's a most placid moose."

"Let's go and find them," suggested Beryl.

Don put his pack set on his back, and we set off in single file with Don in the lead, stopping from time to time as he disentangled his aerial from the branches.

"I've got a terrific reception now," Don whispered. "I think that they are still in the same place."

We could all hear the beeping in the headphones. "We'll go very quietly," Barry whispered, "I really want to see what they are doing."

We moved stealthily forward a few steps at a time, like a patrol approaching an enemy position. A little further on, the tracking collar was lying on the path, where it had been beeping away for the past few hours, but Greedy was long gone. Barry took the collar back to the workshop for further modification, and by the time we got it on Greedy's neck again it was dark. Barry wanted to be back in Edmonton again next morning, but he wished to have another go at checking the behaviour of the moose with the "beeps" on his set.

"I'd like to get up really early," he told us "so that I can start tracking them by daylight."

We heard Barry and Don moving about downstairs before dawn. Beryl and I went down to give them a cup of coffee before they set off. They were in all the equipment that they intended to wear in the north of Alberta that winter and looked like two astronauts about to step onto the moon. Don already had his pack on and his aerial up.

"Splendid reception again this morning," he told us.

The sky was beginning to pale. They finished their coffee and moved to the sliding doors. Barry slid one back, while Don, bent low so that the aerial would clear the top of the door, he stepped out. He straightened up and found himself, like a lance-corporal parading his section, confronted by a row of five moose, who had been standing at the terrace wall hoping that someone might give them some bread.

"Oh hell!" said Barry. "No wonder we had good reception. I guess we'd better give it up. At least we know that the collars are too small, and that the equipment works."

Stuart returned unannounced one wet night. Beryl and I were awakened by the deep burbling of a motorcycle. We found Stuart astride his machine, a two cylinder Triumph, which he had ridden from one of his North American caches. He looked rather dramatic and magnificent, dressed in blue jeans and a white crash helmet, his clothes and his beard running in water since he had just driven through near freezing rain. He glistened in the lamplight like a seal just out of the sea.

Beryl was delighted to have Stuart back and was soon full of plans for his employment. She had been so impressed with the artistry of the collage he had made for her that she now suggested that he should make a mosaic to go under the stove, from broken tiles and china that she had collected. Stuart made a base of plywood to go under the stove, on which he proposed to lay the mosaic. After deep and prolonged thought, he drew his design on the plywood. He then showed it to Beryl for her approval.

"Yes, Stuart. That's splendid," she said, "But what is it? It's the Safeway's store sign, isn't it."

"Aw, Beryl. That's Yin and Yang," he replied.

Stuart continued to work on his design when he had nothing better to do, for the best part of a year, at first with enthusiasm and then with gradual loss of interest, but every small piece of tile was fitted meticulously into place. It included a white seagull, beautifully made of small pieces of tile, which he put in a white background, and a black raven, equally skilfully made, which he put in a black background. He did not mind that the seagull and the raven would never be noticed, so well did they blend with their background.

The roof of the peafowl house had been covered with black tar paper, on the top of which a plaster Buddha perched. It had never been tiled like the swan house. Now a friend, who had just been building a new house, brought us some tiles that had been left over from her roof, most of them cut off from the roof edges. These were nailed on so that they made an adequate roof for the small house, but the finish was rough and irregular. Buddha was given a coat of varnish and perched again, still smiling, on top.

"Come," said Beryl to Stuart, who was laboriously trying to match up the tiles into some appearance of regularity, "Just nail them on any way, as long as they overlap."

"I can't do that," said Stuart. "I haven't got your talent for disorder."

CHAPTER 7

Zeus on the Pond

*"The shadow of the dome of pleasure
Floated midway on the waves"*

ALTHOUGH ZEUS was the first bird on the pond, on the evening that we drove him down from the house, I heard next morning a greater yellow legs, perhaps all the way from Patagonia, proclaiming that the pond was open. Almost at once, the duck began to arrive. Zeus on the pond was much wilder than Zeus in the pen, and he still blamed us for the loss of his mate. For several weeks he would not come for his feed, but swam away when we walked down from the house. From the upstairs window, we could usually see him, wherever he was. He spent a lot of his time with his head down, searching for food on the pond bottom. The rest of his time was spent in preening or resting, either on the water, or on a temporary island, which existed only when the pond was full. He had only been there a few days when we heard his loud trumpeting, and to our delight we saw seven great white swans, circling low above the water.

Zeus, however, had a very different idea about this intrusion. As soon as they were down, at the far end of the pond, he paddled furiously towards them. They did not await his arrival, but took off again, climbing steadily towards the North. We were forlorn that our poor cripple could not accompany them. But not so Zeus. He stood as high as he could in the water, beating his wings and trumpeting, as he proclaimed his delight at their discomfiture. As soon as the raiders had disappeared he settled down again to his humdrum life in the pond, which he now shared with some sycophantic duck, and a pair of muskrats. Next morning a large flock of whistlers flew over, but made no attempt to come down. Zeus answered their wild music, turning his head sideways in between his bouts of trumpeting, so that he could look skywards with one eye, as he did when aircraft came over. He was always aware of anything above him and would see a high flying eagle or a hawk before we did.

One day I saw him examining the dinghy, which was down on the pond again and pulled up on the dam bank. I took his wheat and his special herbivore pellets and put them inside. Zeus, as usual, swam away to the middle of the pond, making his "kek" of suspicion and complaint, but as I left I saw him swim back to the dinghy, heave himself out of the water in his ponderous way, and begin feeding. Thereafter, he became progressively tamer, but it wasn't until August that he took bread again from the hand. The two muskrat also became progressively tamer, and as they saw us arrive with the feed, came arrowing across the pond, often from different directions, paddling earnestly, the black oval tops of their heads and beady black eyes just clear of the surface, their furry backs awash, and their tails lying straight behind. The urgency of their passage sent the ripples spreading to each side. They did not come out while we were there, lying a short stone's throw offshore, nor did they actually steal the food while Zeus was at it for he at times would pursue them, forcing them to dive and disappear. However, they helped themselves directly he was gone. Together with the wild duck they ate most of the feed we brought for Zeus, who was already finding sufficient on the pond bottom and on the shore. The real object of feeding him was to re-establish our friendly relations.

He would allow no swans to come down but did not object to some Canada geese, who arrived and stopped for a few days. Whatever pity we felt for a pinioned bird, he was in infinitely better state than he had been during his miserable, confined winter. May and early June is the best time on the pond. The yellow legs had their nests somewhere in its marshy environs and circled and dived above us, shrieking their repetitive alarm or calling more gently to their mates, "Will you? Will you? Will you?." The snipe were drumming overhead, and there were still plenty of duck halting or not yet nesting, who took wing on our approach. Mallard, pintail and blue-winged teal were like small strings of beads, flung far into the sky. We wanted to call them to come home again, to say that we were leaving. As we left there would be a rush of wings as they crossed high above us, the sun bright on their plumage, and soon they had circled the pond again and were coming in to alight with a splash of water followed by contented quacking. Zeus seemed to enjoy their company and they his. When he had his head down searching the pond bottom, there were always duck close to him as if in the hope of some benefit from the mud that he was disturbing. Resting on the water or on the bank, he usually had birds near him.

Almost the first birds to arrive on the edges of the pond were the red-winged blackbirds, the males before the females. They sat on the bushes calling "chuck" and when they burst into song it was only a three-note affair, "kongkeree, kongkeree," not very lovely, but to those that have sat out the winter with only the "dee, dee, dee" of the chickadees, and the drumming of a hairy woodpecker on the shakes, it was as welcome and as happy a sound as the first notes of the cuckoo in England.

Robins are not plentiful about the game park, but at this time of year there are always a few to welcome the morning with their song of "kill'em, cure'em, give'em physic," as the old settlers interpreted it, or "cheery, cheery, cheerily," which is perhaps a nicer way to tell you that it is time to get up. Round about the pond there is certain to be a killdeer, with its call of "killdee, killdee, killdee," and a red-tailed hawk, scolding from the trees beyond, where a pair habitually make their nest. To hear all these birds, so soon after the ice has thawed, is like sailing into a river from a restless ocean, like stepping suddenly into some other world.

We had no intention of keeping Zeus in lonely celibacy and Ron MacKay had promised us another female when one was available. Plans were started so that the pair could winter on the pond, and for this we had to have some open water. We thought of having an air compressor to blow bubbles out of a pipe as is done sometimes round yachts to keep them ice free. I do not remember why this idea was discarded, but our next plan was to put up a wind-operated propeller on a staging in the deepest part of the lake, so that when the propeller turned it would move the warmer water from the bottom up to the surface. As the wind was not going to blow all the time, we could put an electrically driven propeller on the same staging. This meant taking an underground line from the house to the lake, a distance of about four hundred yards, and then an underwater line to the staging. Near the pond we had an old well that we could use to keep the water well up with an old-fashioned wind-driven pump. If we put in an electrical pump jack, the well could be operated by wind or electricity.

I was away for two months leaving Beryl to implement these plans. With characteristic determination, she set about them. One of the minor setbacks she experienced was when the dinghy upset while transporting angle iron posts to drive into the mud as a base for the staging. It would never have occurred to Beryl to leave them to rot at the bottom of the pond, but any attempt to retrieve them by diving only stirred up an impenetrable cloud of mud.

"I guess the Mounties could get them," suggested Stuart. They have those body snatchers they pull bodies out of lakes with."

Beryl rang up the Mounties in Cochrane.

"Yes, Madam," was the polite reply to her query. "We use small steel grapnels to recover bodies of the drowned. Can we help you?"

Beryl explained her problem.

"They might do the trick all right," said the Mountie laughing. "If you can pick them at the office, I will have them ready for you."

With the help of the body snatchers, the posts were recovered and driven in successfully. By the time I came home, everything was completed and working.

At first Zeus was a little suspicious of the revolving sails that turned the wind-driven propeller but soon he accepted them. In fact, he caused us anxiety by the way he reached down to the propeller, whose movement attracted him to such an extent that we could sometimes hear the rattle of his beak on the blade and had visions of his neck getting caught in it. The muskrats also were delighted with the staging. They found that they could climb out onto a wooden crossbar and would also swim underneath the platform, rather than submerging, to avoid Zeus, who sometimes went after them and once succeeded in catching one momentarily by the tail.

When the lake first froze it looked as if our plans were going to work, as a pool of about twenty feet in diameter remained open. Zeus spent most of his time in or beside the pool, but in order to prevent him from straying too far we surrounded it with some snow fencing. As the weather got colder, the ice began to form each night on the pool, and every morning Stuart, or I, had to break it up. We then scooped up the broken pieces of ice with a landing net and threw them onto the ice behind us, so that a barricade of broken ice built up round the pool. The pond ice on which we stood while doing this was soon two feet thick, a white wall extending downwards against which the ripples lapped, and under which the remains of the lettuce that we brought Zeus were driven by the propeller wash, so that the pool remained clean.

The muskrats were now shore based under the dinghy, which had been turned upside down on the edge of the ice. From there they had a tunnel which led under the ice to the deeper water and so to Zeus's pool. Whenever we fed Zeus, a muskrat would appear in the pool, and although they must have expected to find us in such close proximity, they always dived again with a "plop" when they saw us. As soon as we left, they reappeared to play their game of catch as catch can with Zeus and to grab what feed they could from Zeus's rations.

As the cold increased, we found that the breaking and clearing of ice on Zeus's pool was taking nearly two hours every morning. It was obvious that something else had to be done. Some sort of tent over the pool appeared to be the answer. I was talking to Bill Milne about this, who had been keeping an eye on our efforts with his usual enthusiasm but with some skepticism.

"Now I think you are talking sense," he said. "Have you heard of a 'Pacific Dome?' There's a fellow called Ron Mate that I could put you in touch with. I think that he might be interested in building one. You might want to give it a go."

A "Pacific Dome," we discovered, is a geodetic dome made from varied lengths of two by fours, five lengths being bolted to a centre and the other end of each length being bolted to another centre of five, until, in some mystical manner, a dome is formed, which can be covered with plywood or with fabric. Ron Mate came up to see us. He was an American, a quiet withdrawn man, who spoke little but obviously thought a lot. He was particularly interested in building us a Pacific Dome as he was soon going back to the States, to some rustic and mountainous sanctuary, where he and his family intended to build one for themselves. He said that he'd like to gain the experience in building one by making ours and would do it for us at about cost price. Since he and his son would be doing the work, he told us that there would be little more than the cost of the timber, the plywood centres, the bolts and the fabric. For a twenty-four-foot-diameter dome, twelve feet high and the fabric to cover it, he quoted a very reasonable price.

In a little more than a week, they were ready to start. Ron Mate arrived one evening with all the materials in his truck, which we unloaded onto the ice. Next morning, with his son and daughter and various helpers that we had roped in, all armed with adjustable wrenches and spanners, we set to work. The lower half of the first tier was linked up, making a wavy and unstable circular fence. Ron Mate, like the conductor of an orchestra, kept an eye on all of us, directing us with a spanner in his hand ensuring that we did not bolt the wrong length in the wrong places. As the second and third tiers were built up, the structure became progressively more rigid, until finally the last two by four, with a little pushing and pulling, was forced into place. We then carried the whole dome to the pool, and lifted it, with a struggle, over the wooden staging on which the agitators were mounted. Then, astounded at having erected such an elegant structure in a single day, we went up to the house for a drink.

Zeus had regarded all these goings on with suspicion and while we were putting the dome in place, he waddled off through the snow to a safe distance. He came back in the evening and went into the water. Next day we covered the lower tier with an orange plastic fabric. The colour was a disaster and soon became a reference point for light aircraft which flew in our direction, but the fabric was excellent as it was wind proof, waterproof, and it let in plenty of light. Zeus was left with an open door, and there was room for him to come out on the ice at the edge of the pool. On succeeding days we covered it completely, stapling the fabric down with a staple gun, then nailing light cedar laths over it onto the frame, in order to secure it against the winds. One panel was left open at the top. Most of the stapling of the fabric on the upper tiers was done by Stuart, who sprawled like a long legged spider on top of the frame over the icy pool, his long beard hanging downwards through the structure like a frayed bell rope.

Zeus now had a home and an inside swimming bath, a palace for a swan, and we were no longer bothered by the formation of ice on the pool. The palace would have to be moved before the ice melted, but we left that worry for a later day. Meanwhile Zeus and the muskrats enjoyed his stately pleasure dome and the only thing lacking was a mate. That was about to be put right.

Soon after the construction of the dome was completed Zeus's bride came from the zoo in a sack, and we turned her out in the pool. We called her Io, whom, according to Greek mythology, Zeus loved. Zeus behaved in rather a chauvinistic way, swimming after her and pulling her feathers, but he did not actually attack her. We stayed with them for some time in order to protect her if necessary. When we got back to the house we could see them both sitting outside the door. Io a little behind Zeus.

They spent a great deal of their time in their "stately pleasure dome," but on sunny days they would go on a promenade as far as the dam where they had a better view of the countryside. It was then extremely hard to see them, so perfectly did they match the snow, and we had many frights, thinking perhaps that the coyotes had got them. By the beginning of March the eagles' arrival back in the valley reminded us that soon the ice on the pond would be gone, and we had better think of moving the dome to the shore. Already the ice inside was melting and the edges were under water in some places.

CHAPTER 8

Swans and a Balloon

IT WAS OUR FRIEND and adviser, Bill Milne, who aroused our interest in ballooning. He and Lorraine had made two trips over the Alps from Murren, acting as crew in a friend's gas-filled balloon. Bill told us the story of these two exciting ventures in an amusing self-deprecatory way, as if surprised that such extraordinary things could be happening to him and Lorraine. In one, they made a landing on a steep mountain side in Italy, from where they extricated themselves with difficulty and from which it took three days to recover the balloon. In the other, they had an extremely fast descent from about twelve thousand feet, owing to some defect that had developed in the balloon. It ended in a crash landing, but they were saved from serious injury by jettisoning every available object.

"I saw the altimeter needle going round and round as if it had gone crazy," Bill told us, "but there was really no other way that we could tell that we were falling."

But when they threw out some paper in which their lunches were wrapped, to their surprise they saw the scraps fly upwards and disappear.

"Then we threw out the sandwiches," said Lorraine, "and they just about kept pace with us."

"Then we let go all the sand," added Bill.

"And it got in my hair," continued Lorraine, passing her hand over her lovely auburn head.

When they could see they were about to hit the ground, they threw out the heavier objects, the radio set and the champagne, and they crashed within a ring of this jettisoned debris, badly shaken up but otherwise undaunted.

Bill's only other flight had been in a hot-air balloon from a rally at Calgary. A strong wind had come up, and they had done about fourteen miles before the pilot risked a landing.

"By then," said Bill, "we must have been doing nearly twenty miles an hour, and when we landed we were just tearing along, across a field, scattering cattle, through a barbed wire fence, until the balloon deflated.

"We are starting a balloon club in Calgary now," Bill told us. "I think that you should give it a whirl. You'd enjoy it."

We joined the club, which was being organized by a young engineer. He was the sort of person that had to be organizing something, but who did it quietly and efficiently. He was totally interested in ballooning, its history, its ethics, and its modern practice. He was of the same breed as the Montgolfiers, bearded, precise, well-mannered and scientific. One could imagine him, stepping out of his machine that had appeared so silently from the clouds, to the wonderment of the peasants and the natives, and then proceeding to pop a champagne cork.

As yet we had no balloon but we had numerous meetings which Beryl and I found rather trying, not being very keen on meetings that are held forty miles away, but eventually Bill was selected to do a course at Coeur d'Alene in the U.S.A. so that we might have an instructor. He was soon back ready to take the examination for his licence, with ideas about what sort of balloon should be bought.

Beryl and I had our first experience with hot-air balloons at another Calgary International Rally, when the members of our embryo club were asked to assist at the launchings. About fifteen balloons were competing in a hare and hound race. In this competition the hare starts off first and when he lands, the competitors have to come down as near to him as possible, the winner being the one that lands nearest to the hare. We helped with one balloon at the start, holding it as steady as possible by a light rope to its top, while others held onto its sides and the pilot heated the air inside with great gouts of flame from a propane gas burner fixed above the basket. All the balloons were soon up and away on a light northerly wind which carried them over Calgary, at different altitudes, at varying speeds owing to the difference in wind strength at the selected altitudes. They did not always go in exactly the same direction since the wind currents seemed to vary as much as those of the sea. We followed them by car until the hare landed, and then walked across the fields to see the others come in.

There is something special about balloons. The first that I ever saw was in 1916, at my preparatory school near Harrow, with the army occupants hurriedly jettisoning sand, so that, to our great disappointment, the balloon just cleared the tops of the trees round the playing field and drifted out of sight. Since then, in fact since the Charles hydrogen balloon, which first flew in 1783, there has been little change in design, although a great change in fabrics. There has been more change in the hot-air balloons, in their heating apparatus, which in the Montgolfier's balloon, also first flown in 1783, consisted in burning straw and faggots. When sparks set the fabric smouldering, the fire was put out with a wet sponge on the end of a stick.

Balloons are still a rarity, still a superb sight, so large, so silent, so far removed from the busy world below. Aircraft, which in my boyhood were rare and exciting sights, barely attract a glance, but everyone looks at a balloon and no one knows where it will land. On this day, when the many coloured "hounds" came panting in, the sough of their burners sounding every fifty seconds or so, like porpoises at sea, they were a romantic and enthralling sight.

One day the club balloon arrived. It was coloured red and yellow, as had been the Charles balloon. It was as restless during inflation as a three-year-old horse before a gallop, so that we feared that the brand-new fabric might be burned. The first flights were tethered flights from a small park in the centre of Calgary, with Bill Milne as our instructor, wearing a strange blue cap and full of élan as he yodelled from aloft to the handlers below. He reminded us, however, that we were dealing with a flying machine that could come down with a bang if basic rules were ignored. When summer came, the red-and-yellow balloon was seen further afield over many rancher's fields, but the difficulty with a young balloon club is that there are many applicants for a ride and only one balloon, and the weather around Calgary usually only permits one flight before the wind gets too strong.

On one flying day, we met Stan, a sturdy bush pilot from the north, used to flying his aircraft in the worst weather with few navigational aids. I should have thought that he would have had enough excitement in the air, but he had never been up in a balloon and was mad keen to go. He was going to fly on that day with Del Michaud, who was down from Edmonton, and had recently got his licence. The inflation, early one morning, in a little valley north of Cochrane, had been uneventful, and as the balloon rose above the valley it seemed to hang suspended, as if undecided as to which direction it would take, but once out of the shelter of the valley sides, it took off towards the north.

"Look at the way he's moving now," said Bill, who was driving one of the chase cars in which I was riding. Half an hour later, we were driving up a road directly under the balloon, so that we could check its speed on the car's speedometer. It appeared to be doing just twenty miles an hour.

"It looks like a rough landing," said Bill.

The balloon was descending slowly and we were able to get ahead of it close to the pilot's selected landing point. Del had chosen a field where the hay bales were stacked, coming in very low and steady, but when he touched down, the flimsy plywood and canvas "basket" went onto its side, and the two occupants, clinging to its framework, had a rough ride for fifty yards over the grass. Bill, showing a great turn of speed, was able to catch hold of them and slow their progress until the balloon was deflated. Two grinning faces then appeared, none the worse for their sleigh ride. Stan was so delighted with his adventure that he determined there and then to get a balloon of his own.

After his next tour in the North he appeared again, this time as the owner of a very fine balloon. It was much more powerful than the club balloon, but before he could fly it in free flight, he had first to get his ballooning licence. Bill and Beryl, meeting him one day in Calgary, were listening to his description of the new balloon. This was just when we were wondering how we would move Zeus's dome from the ice before it melted.

"I've got an idea, Stan," said Beryl. "Why don't we have a meet at the house and you could pick up the dome for us and move it?"

Bill, always game for something like this, and a great proponent of the idea of moving arctic gas by dirigible, added support.

"You could do it easily with your balloon," he said. "The dome can't weigh more than about 600 pounds."

"I haven't got my flying licence yet," replied Stan, "but I could do it on a tethered flight, if it hasn't got to move too far."

"Only to the edge of the pond. About fifty yards," said Beryl, eagerly. "That's splendid. Let's fix it for next Sunday. You come the day before and stay the night at the house so that you can see what has to be done."

On Saturday Beryl, Stuart, and I fixed two lengths of rope over the dome and made fast the four ends on the bottom at opposite sides. Then we fastened a lift from these ropes, where they crossed at the centre and brought it down to the ground, so that it could be attached to a lift rope from the balloon. Stan arrived late in the evening but still full of confidence when he surveyed the task ahead of him.

We were up for breakfast early next morning. Although March was more than half gone, the snow was still deep. The Chinook winds had melted the surface which had frozen again at night into a stiff crust, a crust that would barely support a dog and made all movement difficult. Only around the boles of the trees was there dead grass showing, as well as in a few places on southern slopes and ridges, so that the country looked at its worst, wearing a patchwork coat of old snow and brown grass. The aspen trees were still stark and leafless, but on Sunday morning I could see that the topmost twigs were moving. We rang up the weather office. The winds were calm in Calgary, always a little different from where we are, but they were expected to blow from seven to ten miles an hour in the morning and fifteen in the afternoon. Too strong to launch a balloon. Stan kept stepping outside while we had breakfast, holding his finger to the wind. I could see that once started on a job like this he would be a hard man to stop. The wind was about three to five miles an hour, just sufficient to stir the trees.

"We don't have to do it," I told him.

"No," he said, "I'm sure that it's going to be all right. We'll have a go."

Then there was a rush to get everything done before the wind strengthened. The Balloon Club members had to be told that the lift was on and other help had to be roped in. David Lowall, a doctor, said he'd come with his son Mark, and I rang up Jim Kerfoot, my rancher neighbour, who was always game for some excitement and said he'd be up directly, as I knew he would, with his young and active sons, Hamish and Quentin.

Before long we had about twenty people ready to help in the inflation and all went down to the pond. A heavy truck was driven out onto the ice and a strong nylon strap, about a hundred yards in length was laid out from it to the basket, so that when the dome was lifted, with the tether truck moving, or paying out the strap, the balloon could be moved to the right position, and then allowed to sink until the dome was on the ground.

Stan was as eager as a hound on a hot scent. The balloon was unpacked and unrolled on the snow until it seemed to cover an acre of ground. Assistants were told their various duties. Stan was to be accompanied by two newcomers to the Balloon Club, both dressed in black overalls with the Balloon Club badge on the sleeve. Their outfits made up for any deficiency in experience. The basket was attached to the rigging and, fortunately as it was to turn out, this balloon had a real wicker basket. As the last small shackle was fastened, a sudden cold and rather strong wind stirred the green fabric. I had a feeling of misgiving and said to Stan, "You know, you don't have to do it just because all these people are here."

"I know," he said, "but I'd just like to try an inflation anyway."

The air blower, a motor-driven fan, was pulled into position and switched on. Two tall members of the Balloon Club held the mouth of the balloon open. The fan was directed towards the mouth, and the fabric began to roll restlessly as if the balloon were waking from sleep. With the basket on its side, Stan crouched behind his burners like a soldier behind his machine gun. The gas was lit by a spark from a flint while he waited for the first opportunity to send in a blast of flame. The fabric billowed and swelled with the fan-driven air, and then there was a roar from the burners as Stan saw his chance for releasing a gush of flame without burning the fabric.

This and the landing are the most exciting times in ballooning. The fan is switched off and the blasts from the burner become more frequent and more prolonged as the air is heated in the balloon, and the danger from a burn becomes less. The envelope fills, rolls, and billows, still held down by hands at its sides and by a rope from the peak. Gradually it begins to rise, and as it does so the pilot raises the basket so that the flame from the burners strikes into the centre of the orifice. His crouching position, his tense uplifted face, framed by his helpers on either side, and the great gouts of flame from the burner, all go to make a splendid action picture. When the balloon is inflated, and riding above the basket, and the pilot is inside testing for buoyancy, there is a sudden relief from tension.

Stan achieved his inflation without accident, and soon the great green balloon was riding quietly above the basket, competing with the orange fabric of the dome as the only gay colour for miles around. He kept the burners going only enough to keep the fabric inflated and the basket on the ground while his black-overalled companions climbed in. One or two blasts from the burners, and then he felt the basket lift slightly. Stan gave another blast and then called, "Hands off." The basket rose gently to a height of about ten feet. All seemed to be well.

At this moment, a cold gust of wind, far in excess of anything that had blown that morning, leapt over the trees to the west, bounced off the ice on the pond, and swept the balloon into the air. The tether strap tightened, the basket was pulled away at a conforming angle, and then there was a resounding crack as the strap broke and the basket swung back, with twenty feet of its broken strap dangling below. The balloon was away — away except for the unhappy people hanging on to its guide ropes, which were not meant to hold a runaway balloon and were far too thin for hands to hold under the strain. They hung on gallantly, stumbling, falling, groaning, and being dragged along the ice until they had all let go, the last of them hitting the dam wall in a horizontal position and burying his head in the snow.

We watched dismayed, as the balloon, with its unwilling occupants and without a flying licence, headed for Calgary. It soon began to sink until it looked as if the basket, still going at a good pace, would never clear the game-park fence. At the last moment, it lifted again but fifty yards further on struck the ground, throwing Stan, the pilot, out. Stan bounced to his feet and was off like a buffalo through the snow in pursuit of his expensive balloon. Lightened by the loss of Stan's not inconsiderable weight, it bounded away again and after another seventy yards the basket once more struck the ground, jettisoning a black figure, who lay still. Finding itself still further lightened the balloon took off once more until the basket hit the ground for the third time, shedding its last occupant who also lay still on the ground. The path of the balloon was beginning to look like a battlefield.

The onlookers surged forward as best they could through the snow, towards the fence. The first over were the young, Hamish and Quentin Kerfoot, Mark Lowell, and Stuart. Beryl, who is ageless, was there, and Mark's father, David, the doctor. I confined my assistance to standing on the fence and shouting, "Run, Stuart, run," being quite convinced that at his age, I should have run faster. Near me a girl was hanging onto the fence, the wife of one of the fallen, her eyes wide, as she said, "Oh, no, oh, no!" I thought involuntarily of Mrs. Ramsbottom as Albert disappeared down the lion's mouth.

Stan ploughed on, ignoring the bodies on the ground, until he had the broken strap in his hands. He was dragged along the ground until help arrived. The doctor stopped to give aid to the fallen, but the others soon tailed on to the strap, and Stan was at last able to get to the basket and pull the rip cord. They were just in time as otherwise the balloon might have reached the trees and done itself some damage.

Jim and I, the two old soldiers, set off in his four-wheel-drive truck to find a way into the field, so that we might remove the injured. We had not gone far before we stuck in the snow and spent the next half hour digging ourselves out. When we got back, rather ashamed of our absence from the battlefield, we found that the wounded had already been evacuated by ladders placed against the fence.

"They will be all right," David told us. "No serious damage."

Those that remained of our force went back to the house for a drink and some of Beryl's strong soup that always seems to appear in an emergency. With this under his belt, Stan, whose hands had been quite badly cut by the strap that he had hung onto with such determination, suggested that we should move the dome by hand. We trooped back to the pond, picked up the dome with comparative ease, and carried it back to the shore, which I suppose we might have done in the first place. The swans, sitting out on the ice, had paid little attention to all this activity, but now, when a small red aircraft flew over, they both got to their feet and trumpeted loudly. That night they went back to the pool, and the two injured balloonists came back from hospital. As is common in most balloon misfortunes, they had suffered little more than a severe shaking up. Stan was the sort of hardy person that would have to fall from a ten-storey building before he received a shaking and was soon flying his balloon again, but with a licence.

Stuart, who had been with us so long now, felt the call of the birds winging north on migration and he himself drifted away. He left some old clothes and two white helmets in a cardboard box under his bed. His large motorcycle, which was suffering from some minor complaint, sat in the barn. One day, no doubt, he will be back to reclaim them.

CHAPTER 9

Petruska in Trouble

SPRING CAME QUICKLY after Stuart left. All the ice disappeared from the pond. Zeus and Io, like two great cruise ships in a foreign port, surrounded by tugs, tenders, and bumboats, floated majestically, accompanied by their following of wild duck. When we walked down to feed them bread, they paddled eagerly towards the shore, and on reaching shallower water hoisted themselves up onto their legs and waddled, black booted, towards us. They accepted the bread greedily, but at the same time they hissed their disapproval of this invasion of their precincts. On the edge of the pond the yellow legs started their piping and dived on us in mock attack, while on the dam a kildeer took up the complaint and at times fluttered along the ground, dragging a wing, to persuade us away from her nest. All the trees had burst into leaf. It was time for Petruska to have her calf.

In January she had been big with calf. I had made a bet with Beryl that she would have twins, but Beryl put her money on a singleton. One day, towards the end of May, she failed to come to the house. Beryl started her usual anxious peregrinations. For my part, I was worried on Beryl's account, never fully trusting Petruska at this time.

After she had been missing for a day, Beryl disappeared for two hours in search of Petruska. Just after I had decided that I had better go and find out what Beryl was doing, I saw her coming back from the woods, a plastic bucket of feed in her hand. She was walking so listlessly that I knew at once that she had failed in her search.

"I can't find her anywhere," she said. "She's in none of her old places."

"Both sides?" I asked.

"Yes. Both sides, of course," she replied impatiently. "I saw Pollux," she continued, relenting. "He was down by the gate, so I don't think she's there. Tonight I'll have a really good look on the west side. It's so thick there that I may have missed her."

The evening search was equally fruitless, and next morning Beryl was off immediately after breakfast. She was back before an hour was up, and again her step told me immediately how she had fared.

"I've found her," she called. "She's got one calf. No wonder that I could not find her. She's right on the edge of the aspen on the northeast side, and there's no water near. I am sure she can be seen from the road. And near her, I found the most extraordinary little thing on the ground. It looks like a moose embryo. I'm going to go back and get it. I am sure that Val Geist will be interested. I'll take a plastic bag."

Off she went again and was soon back with a skinny little embryo moose in her plastic bag. It weighed about six pounds and was hairless and almost fleshless so that the skeletal bones, joints, and sinews were all obvious.

"How is Petruska?" I asked.

"She hasn't eaten anything, but I think she's all right. The calf is standing up, and she's licking it, but I don't know whether it's suckled yet. Petruska always looks awful at this time of year anyway, with her winter coat dropping out. We'll have to take her some water. I'm going to put this in the deep-freeze."

Petruska has always had her calves within easy reach of water, but this time she was a long way from it and in a very public place, compared to her usual secret hide-outs. We loaded the Landrover with water containers and a large plastic bowl and drove to Petruska. She was still at the edge of the aspens on the other side of a grassy hollow, with a small chestnut calf lying beside her. We took the bowl down to the hollow, where she could see what we were doing without being disturbed, and there filled it with water. That night Beryl telephoned Val Geist.

"That is most interesting," said Val. "How old do you think it is?"

"I haven't a clue," Beryl replied. "It weighs about six pounds, I should guess."

"Splendid," said Val. "About three to four months, I suppose. She was probably reabsorbing it. Now can you preserve it? That is most important. Have you a deep-freeze?"

Beryl's and Val's minds seem to run on parallel lines as far as moose are concerned, and she was able to tell him that it was already in the freezer.

We often have gophers for the foxes in the deep-freeze as well as rabbits and guinea pigs (used rabbits and guinea pigs) from the biological department of the university. Now they were joined by an embryo moose. We agreed that the bet was off.

For the next two days Petruska remained in the same place and neither ate the feed that Beryl brought, nor drank the water from the bowl. "She seems listless," said Beryl, anxiously, "and the calf is not looking too good either. I'm certain she's sick. I am going to ring up that wild animal vet that we heard of from Kenya who teaches at the Saskatoon Veterinary College. What was his name? Jerry Haigh, wasn't it?"

She telephoned him that night. He said that Petruska might have a puerperal infection but that he'd have to examine her before he could give any advice. He agreed to fly over next morning, and I recognised him easily at the airport although I had never met him before. Somehow we must have collected the same tribal markings. Both Beryl and I had been to Kenya, so that we had common acquaintances, and soon felt as if we had known him for years.

He brought with him a long blow pipe with which to propel a tranquilizing dart, should it be necessary to put Petruska down for his examination.

"It is much better than a gun," he told us. "Much less distressing for the animal. There is no noise, no shock and no bruising. They think a fly has bitten them, but you have to get within thirty feet to hit them."

In case Petruska objected to his near approach, he suggested that, while Beryl talked to her, I might use the blow pipe to tranquilize her. He gave it to me for one or two practice shots. Full of confidence that I could blow the dart for at least thirty feet, I filled my lungs, pointed the blow pipe at a door about thirty feet away, and blew a great blast. To my surprise the dart trickled out of the end of the pipe and fell to the ground.

"You have to sort of spit into it, as you do when blowing a hunting horn or a bugle," said Jerry, laughing.

My next effort was successful, and I was soon hitting the door approximately in the middle.

"I think Petruska may be a little better," said Beryl, "but she still hasn't eaten any of the feed. However, she had a good drink of water from the bowl last night. The calf still looks very shaky."

"We may not have to put her out," said Jerry, "and before I do anything I'd like to have a good look at her, if I can get close enough. I suggest that you, Beryl, go up to her as you usually do and talk to her. Then I'll come up slowly, talking to you, and perhaps she won't mind me coming up to you."

We walked over to the hollow and stayed to one side, while Beryl went up to Petruska with her bucket of feed and fondled her. Both Petruska and the calf were on their feet, the calf close behind Petruska. She looked mildly across at Jerry and me, her big ears pricked while Beryl stroked her neck. Jerry started off towards her, while I took up a position on a flank. Jerry moved quietly towards Beryl, talking as he went, but when he was still fifty yards away Petruska put her ears back. Jerry halted, and the ears came forward again. He set off once more, but Petruska had had enough. She pinned down her ears and paced angrily towards him, leaving Beryl with the calf.

Jerry had chosen his route with one eye on a large spruce tree, which he now made haste to get behind. Petruska followed round then doubled back to meet him, but Jerry, used to similar adventures with rhino, was too quick for her and kept the tree between them. Petruska then made an attempt to dive through the tree, her head coming out of the branches on the same side as Jerry, but since the branches were low and spreading, her legs failed to make similar progress, and she was temporarily hung up. Jerry took this opportunity to reach the other side of the hollow, doing the fifty yards in about five seconds. Petruska extricated herself from the tree and returned to Beryl and her calf.

Beryl rejoined us, and Jerry, barely out of breath, gave us his opinion. "If that moose was in a zoo," he said, "I'd tranquilize her and do something for her fever, but now that I have seen her, I think that she is wild enough and has sufficient resilience to recover on her own. Perhaps the best treatment that we can give her is to leave her alone, but it is quite possible that she won't have another calf next year."

"I'd like her to have a rest anyway," said Beryl. "That's her eighth calf in five years."

Petruska's calf was a very shy and gentle female. Petruska, as Jerry had foreseen, recovered quickly. The milk flowed and the calf grew splendidly, as if to make up for its initial setback. We called her "Simplicity."

It was June. In the afternoons, majestic thunderheads towered in the distance like some great Himalayan range divided by rifts and glaciers. In some direction or other, not very far away on those thundery afternoons, there was sure to be a storm lowering, with lightning boring down to the ground in something more than a flash, but rather a relentless attack. Against this blackness overhead, and in sunlight away from the path of the storm, a white farmhouse may stand out like a beacon, with grass, still uncut, young aspen leaves, and the new growth on the spruce trees around it, shining a brilliant green.

That year we had a drought. Although the sky was continuously overcast, the country was dull with the insignificant rain, which failed to check the rapid descent of the water table. It could not compare with the exuberant discharge of one thunderstorm, which in a few minutes leaves the ditches overflowing. The water receded all round the shores of the pond, leaving wide expanses of drying mud. The wild duck, when they brought their young from the nest to the water, had no cover available at the water's edge. There were several broods as usual, which we saw swimming close behind their mothers, but gradually they fell prey to marsh harriers and other hawks until they were nearly all gone. Finally I saw three bufflehead ducklings alone on the water while the duck sat on an up-turned dinghy some distance away, as if, for lack of food and cover, she was making plans to desert them. Next time I was down on the pond, they had all disappeared. Coming down the drive now, we no longer saw a wide expanse of water, and half the life of the place seemed to have gone.

In order that we should not again have trouble with Zeus's dome sinking on melting ice, we dug a large hole in the shore of the lake just above the water line of wet years, and we filled this with water by pumping from the well. In this we again set up an electrically driven agitator, and then put the dome over the top. We thought that Zeus and Io would now have a pool for the winter. The swans immediately accepted their new house and spent their nights in the water, which, driven by the agitator, swirled and eddied about them.

Some years before, Chris and Betty Harvey had come to the house, two young and adventurous people, about to set out on a world tour. They intended to travel on foot, on bicycle, by bus, and by train, in fact on any form of transport, the cheaper the better, that enabled them to see the country. Now they were back, loaded with happy experiences and facing once more the necessity of working for a living. They were both extremely proficient in their jobs, he a chemical engineer and she a highly qualified secretary. They were trying to find some compensation for the ending of their nomad life by looking for a home in the country.

Whenever Beryl and I drove down Grand Valley, she used to look across at an old log cottage, almost lost in surrounding ranch buildings and apparently in disuse.

"I'd like to get hold of that cottage," was always Beryl's theme as we drove past. "We really want another house in case we get someone to help us with the reserve and we'll have to do that soon. I wonder if it could be moved, and if the owners would sell it."

"What on earth do you want with an old ruin like that," I asked.

"I like it," she replied. "The trouble with you is that you have no vision." Now Chris and Betty's dilemma, the search for an inexpensive house in the country, put spurs to her intent.

"If we bought it and moved it, would you like to live in it and do the work instead of rent?" she asked them. They said that they would, and Beryl spoke to Bruce Boothby, the rancher who owned it.

"I've been meaning to get rid of it for years," he told her, "but I haven't liked the idea of pulling it down because of its history. It was built for Donald and Jane Morrison around the turn of the century. You can have it for nothing if you can get it moved. I'd like to build a corral there."

Anything built round the turn of the century is an historical monument in Alberta. John Morrison came out from South Uist first in 1887. He returned to South Uist in 1895 to bring out his bride. The new house was then built, a two-storeyed log house with the logs dovetailed at the corners. Beryl got in touch with York Shaw, who is a specialist in the moving of historical buildings.

He came out to look at the house and, to my surprise, said that it could be moved if the newer extensions at each end were first pulled down. A month later, the whole remaining house was slid onto a trailer and moved ten miles to its new site, pursued by confused sparrows and swallows, which had made their nests in the eaves. The new place for the "Morrison house" had first been chosen by the horses, who liked to stand on a small knoll, sheltered by an aspen copse from the cold north wind where they were in sunshine for most of the short winter days. It also had a good view of the mountains, which perhaps the horses didn't appreciate.

The house was put onto a concrete foundation, and fourteen logs, that were found to be rotten, were replaced. The old moss caulking was pulled out and the logs were recaulked with styrofoam and sealed on the inside with Tremco, a flexible rubbery substance. The outside, between the logs, was filled with cement, as had been the practice when the house was built.

By Christmas, Betty and Chris had moved in. Perhaps because of their own warm personalities, perhaps because the old house had an aura of its own, there was always a sense of welcome, comfort, and peace within its doors, although the plumbing was not yet fixed and hot water came from the kitchen stove. I had to admit that I had been lacking in "vision" in this respect, and it is good to think that the old house, once built with such pride and care, is once more occupied.

Someone else had also been looking for a home for the winter. One evening, at dusk, while I was looking through my window at the fox pens, I saw a strange black object moving down the fence on the inside of the run. At first I could not make out what it was, but, with the help of my field glasses, saw that it was a large skunk. The foxes steered clear of him, and his slow progress made me think of a haughty Spanish caballero in a black poncho, out for his "paseo." He was very well set up for the winter, as he was living on the fox's food and in one of the earths that they had dug.

Outside the run we also found fox tracks in the snow. Thinking that it might be Josephine, who had been away for more than a year, we set a trap for her. The traps that we use for recapturing the foxes when they get out of the runs (they are very adept at this) are wire traps with spring doors at each end. Both doors can be left open to accustom the fox to going through the trap, or the trap can be set, so that one door is open which closes when the fox steps on a plate inside the trap. I have often seen a fox set off a trap. They never seem to be alarmed and usually, after a short period of investigation, they settle down to eat the bait. The traps are used sometimes for purposes of identification and sometimes in order to transfer a fox from one run to another as well as to recover those that manage to get out, but (fortunately) stay close to the runs. Some foxes have been caught several times, and these now try to pull the bait towards them by reaching with a fore-paw through the wire mesh of the trap without going inside. In doing this, they are apt to release the spring so that the door shuts, and they can then work undisturbed on pulling the bait through the mesh.

One morning I looked out of my bedroom window and saw a skunk in the trap.

"My God!" I called to Beryl, "We've got a skunk in the trap. Now what are we going to do?"

We planned the skunk operation over breakfast. Dressing for the fray, we put on our old sailing oilskins pulling plastic bags over our shoes, and finishing off, in order to keep the skunk's spray out of our hair and eyes, with sou'westers and sunglasses. Betty Harvey came to see the fun, and from one side called the shots as I advanced, holding a plastic sheet in front of me. Beryl followed close behind with a length of rope. I was in need of Betty's assistance, because wearing dark glasses and holding a sheet in front of me, I could not see where I was going and was liable to fall over the trap.

"He's fired once," Betty called, "He's fired twice. I can see his tail jerk. Three yards to go to the trap."

When I could feel the trap with my foot I bent down and wrapped the plastic sheet around the cage while Beryl quickly secured it with rope. I began to feel that we had been overdoing the caution, and although the smell of skunk hung around us and was particularly strong when we got into the truck to drive him away, I did not find it very offensive. We drove the skunk away for about ten miles, and then shook it out onto the side of the road between trees. Without a parting shot, it cantered away into the forest. Its gait was slow and clumsy, and I felt sorry to see it go, so alone and unprotected until it had recharged its magazine. We wondered how it would survive in such a bleak and barren land, and what it would find to eat.

We caught several skunk like this and became quite expert in dealing with them. On occasions, passing travellers would be surprised to see two people dressed as for heavy seas getting out of a truck halted beside the road. The oilskins soon lost their smell when hung on a clothes line. We caught the Spanish gentleman in the run by making a chicken wire tunnel from the hole that he was using to the trap, in order to prevent the foxes from stealing the bait or getting caught first. The moose appeared and watched through the game-park fence which makes one of the walls of the fox runs. They pressed against the fence with great interest as I advanced behind my sheet, but at the first shot from the skunk, they took off at a gallop.

Our last skunk was caught outside in a trap set near the path that leads to Kochi's kennel. In her old age she is not as alert as she used to be and was unaware of the skunk as she walked towards the kennel in the early morning. As she received the skunk's fire she winced like a frigate receiving a broadside. That night she insisted on sleeping in my bedroom. I had a marvellous night, as if I had some sleep-inducing inhaler which kept my nasal passages clear.

There were many ponds and sloughs empty because of the drought, and it was a common sight to see drilling rigs trying for new water. Everywhere the water table was down, and there was no promise for the future as there had been little snow. We managed to keep the water in the newly dug hole under the dome at the right level by almost continuous pumping from the well beside it. Zeus and Io seemed to be happy and usually spent the night in the water. Because of the movement of the water caused by the agitator, we had to fasten snow fencing underwater round the edges of the pool to prevent erosion of its banks.

On sunny days, Zeus and Io would go for long walks in the snow, but if it was cold they stayed in the water or at the entrance to the dome. They could not venture far because it was too cold for their feet, and every few yards of progress necessitated a halt while they sat down, carefully tucking their black feet under their wings while they waited for them to warm up before moving on.

Beryl and I were spending the night in Calgary while Chris and Betty looked after the animals. That evening Beryl received an urgent message to telephone Betty at our house. All sorts of dire possibilities crowded into Beryl's head as she made the call; the foxes escaped, the moose gone, a fire put out, or old Kochi collapsed. But it was none of these.

"Hello Betty, did you want me to call you?"

"I was so worried, I had to call you. I've just been down to the swans."

A coyote or a lynx has got them, thought Beryl, but it wasn't that either.

"They've got cold feet," said Betty anxiously.

In January the well ran dry, but the pool continued to gulp water. In order to keep it full enough for the swans to get in and out, we had to take from four to six forty-five gallon drums of water from the house, every day, and siphon the water into the pool. This took just as long and was as cold a job as that of a rancher who daily has to feed 200 cows at this time of year. The cows at least appreciate the truck which spills out their hay or silage, but the swans regarded our arrival twice a day with indifference. However, they were our responsibility, and we had to do the best that we could for them.

Long before there was any hope of the ice melting so that the swans could go back to the pond, a letter arrived from the Wildlife Service drawing our attention to a new regulation to the effect that no captive birds or birds reared in captivity might be released to the wild. This regulation was to prevent the spread of duck enteritis, which was prevalent in some captive flocks.

Our object in keeping Zeus and Io was that they might breed and that their young might help to re-establish the old flight paths across the prairie, even if it meant that their first southerly migration had to be done on wheels. We thought that the old birds would drive their last year's young away from the pond to neighbouring sloughs in the spring and that the onset of cold weather would drive them south in the fall. It would have been interesting to see.

The straw that broke the camel's back was a request for a ten-dollar fee for a licence to keep waterfowl. Since the birds belonged to the government, and as we had spent so much time and money in an effort to help further the preservation of trumpeters, this request was too much to be borne with equanimity, and we asked for them to be taken back. They are now in the Saskatoon Zoo where, in the winter at any rate, they must be more comfortable than they were here and their sicknesses, if any, can be cured by our friend Jerry Haigh.

The trumpeters were lovely birds to have on the pond in summer, with their wild discordant trumpeting as an aircraft flew over, but every time that they spread their pinioned wings, we felt reproach. Beryl and I decided never again to have pinioned birds and to keep only endangered animals (apart from the moose) who were at home in the cold winter.

Our decision sealed the fate of the peafowl who rarely come out of their house during the winter and suffer from frostbite if caught by a cold wind. The lovely blue-shouldered peacock, whose call so often rejoiced me in summer, had been taken by a lynx or coyote, after surviving these dangers for six years. His two drab hens both lost their broods to predators, one of whom was Kochi. Rather than see them suffer through another cold winter, and since they were young enough to make excellent eating, they were condemned by the worst predator of all — the pot.

Meanwhile Simplicity had grown up into a fine and gentle moose. Petruska had suffered no permanent ill effects from Simplicity's birth, and now we could see that she was in calf again. Simplicity was destined for the Lion Safari Park, at Rockton, near Toronto, where a new "drive through" section had been arranged for Canadian animals. One day we heard from Colonel Dailley, the director, that a trailer was on its way to pick her up. We opened the gates into the drive so that we might have a small area in which to prepare Simplicity for boxing. For this purpose we had made a mock travelling box. Petruska, delighted at being allowed to revisit an area that had been closed to her for some time, immediately led Simplicity into the drive. By the evening, Petruska wanted to go out again. We allowed her through the gates, but kept Simplicity in the drive. Neither of them seemed to be unduly upset by this separation, nor did we have any difficulty in teaching Simplicity to go in and out of the box.

When the trailer arrived, it was as different from the training box as could be: a large metal affair, normally used for shipping horses. It was cavernous and noisy, and smelt strongly of its recent occupants. It had, however, a low sill and a wide rear door. It was backed up to a low rise at the west end of the house, but Beryl and I doubted that Simplicity would even venture near it.

Bernie and Pam, the two drivers, were anxious to load the moose as soon as possible, and to get off to Edmonton where they had more animals to collect. I believe that they had expected Simplicity to be ready for them in a corral, from where she could be hustled without delay into the trailer. Bernie was a sturdy young man, built like a Sumo wrestler, with a stomach beginning to overhang his belt. He was full of a chauvinistic confidence that would do little to reassure a young moose. Pam, on the other hand, was a tall good-looking girl, a gray-eyed Athena, yet so gentle and sympathetic that she immediately won Beryl's trust, and she stopped worrying about how well Simplicity would be looked after during the long journey, if and when we got her loaded.

Simplicity soon appeared at the house. She was eager enough for her food, but not to such an extent that she'd follow Beryl into the trailer. After many attempts we decided that Bernie and Pam would have to stay the night. They had transferred their bags into their room, and I was looking out of the window upstairs, waiting for them to come up for supper, when I saw Simplicity looking at her feed bowl, which Beryl had placed well within the cavernous trailer. Suddenly she made up her mind, stepped carefully in, and disappeared from view. I was aghast at the missed opportunity, but as I turned, hoping to be able to do something about it, I saw Bernie tiptoeing like a thief in the night round the corner of the house. Then, with remarkable speed and agility for such a solid man, he leapt for the door and slammed it shut. Without giving Bernie and Pam any supper, we loaded their suitcases into the truck and hurried them on their way, since movement seems to be the panacea for the nerves of newly-boxed animals.

Next morning we had a telephone call from Pam to say that Simplicity was travelling well, and a few days later another call to say that she had been to visit her at the Safari Park and that she was settling down happily.

In due course, Petruska calved again. She chose the worst kind of weather in which to have her calf. A day of wild winds, rain, and wet snow. Beryl, plodding in search of her, the feed bucket in one hand and the other as deep in a pocket as it would go, her shoulders shrugged against the cold gusts, came upon the afterbirth. Petruska had always cleaned up her afterbirth, so Beryl wondered whether she was all right, and whether she had had difficulty in calving. Not far away she found her standing in the trees, a healthy bull calf beside her. Because of the weather in which he had been born, we called him "Hardy," and within a few days Beryl had made friends with him.

CHAPTER 10

The Wood Bison

IN NORTH AMERICA, man has shown himself to be a particularly voracious predator. He was responsible for the complete extinction of the passenger pigeons, which used to darken the skies with their flight. Their huge flocks were reduced to one bird, that died in Chicago Zoo in 1914. He was responsible for the near extinction of the bison, of the whooping crane, the trumpeter swan, and other birds and animals including the little swift fox, which we are trying to preserve.

At one time, there are reputed to have been over 60,000,000 head of bison on their vast range, throughout central North America, east of the Rocky Mountains. These bison consisted of two sub-species, the plains bison, rejoicing in the delightful scientific name of *Bison bison bison*, and the wood bison, called *Bison bison athabascae*, which were first seen by Samuel Hearne, on the shores of Great Slave Lake, in 1792. Their habitat then extended through the aspen parklands of Alberta and Saskatchewan from the North Saskatchewan River, north through the coniferous forests as far as Lac La Martre, which lies northeast of Great Slave Lake. It extended westwards to the eastern slope of the Rockies and to the valleys of the great rivers, the Peace and the Liard, which find their sources therein.

When the huge herds of the plains bison were virtually extinct, the dust of their passing laid, the roar of the bulls, like the rumble of breakers on some stormy shore, for ever stilled, the buffalo hunters turned their attention to the wood bison in the northern woods. In a few years, they too were almost destroyed, until in 1893 only about 300 remained in the lower Peace River and the Slave River areas, although there must have still been some scattered groups in the more inaccessible parts of their original range, which were not reported.

Just when their future existence was in doubt, the Canadian government passed a law for their protection in 1893. This was first enforced by the ubiquitous "Mounties," until in 1911 six "Buffalo Rangers" were commissioned for the surveillance of the bison, and in 1923 Wood Buffalo Park was established. This park, of about 17,000 square miles, lies south of the Great Slave Lake and east of the Slave River. By the time the park was created, the herd had increased, due to the care of the Mounties and the Rangers, to about 1500 head. Of the scattered remnants outside the park, the last were finished off by the Indians who destroyed a herd of twenty-eight bison along the banks of the Liard River, in 1926.

Like the horses, that were introduced to America by the Spanish and were soon all over the continent, bison multiply quickly when left alone. This happened to the plains bison in Wainwright Buffalo Park, which had built up from a small herd brought there from Montana between the years 1906 and 1912. These had multiplied to such an extent that in twenty years they were badly over-crowded on their range. In Wood Buffalo Park, there was plenty of room for them and, regardless of the result of mixing two sub-species, and regardless of the fact that some were already infected with tuberculosis and brucellosis, over 6,000 were transferred by rail and barge to Wood Buffalo Park. They were released, between 1925 and 1928, along the banks of the lower Slave River, where they soon mingled and interbred with the wood bison. By 1941 it was estimated that the total park population was about 12,000, with only one or two per cent pure wood bison. The romantic story of the saving of the wood bison sub-species is one of herculean effort, for the handling of these huge self-willed creatures, which can move like a tank when so inclined, is a huge task in itself.

The preservation of the wood bison as a pure species was taken in hand again in 1957. It was hoped that some wood bison might have escaped contact with the plains bison in the comparatively inaccessible northwest corner of the park, and in this year, Doctor Novakowski of the Canadian Wildlife Service, during an aerial count of the bison in the park, discovered their presence in the Nyarling River and the Buffalo Lake areas.

In 1959, after further reconnaissance flights, which had shown that the herd were effectively separated by forest, muskeg, and sand eskers from the other bison in the park, an expedition was organized, under Doctor Novakowski, to make a further study of the herd and to take some specimens. Doctor Novakowski managed to get five specimens, which were later confirmed by the National Museums of Canada as being wood bison. To a non-scientific observer, the two sub-species look much the same, but in general terms the wood bison are larger, have a darker pelage, longer horns, less of a topknot of hair on their heads, and less of a "robe" and "chaps" on their shoulders and forelegs. The robe is dark and more closely matches the body than the golden robe of the plains bulls.

As a result of this confirmation, the Canadian Wildlife Service undertook to move some of the wood bison to an area where contact with the plains bison could be prevented. A trapping corral of twenty acres was built at Needle Lake, near Buffalo Lake, and an additional holding corral was constructed near Fort Smith. In February 1963, seventy-seven wood bison were driven, largely on bulldozed snow roads, into the Needle Lake Corral. Of these, twenty died. It is not known from what cause they died, but probably from a condition induced by the stress of the drive. Of the others, only one was found to have tuberculosis, but fifty-four per cent reacted to the test for brucellosis. Those that were free from the disease were trucked to Fort Smith, and the following summer eighteen were released on a previous bison range, west of Great Slave Lake.

In 1962 anthrax broke out amongst the herds of plains bison outside the park and east of the Slave River. Nearly 300 animals died in three weeks. Efforts were made to burn and bury all the carcasses and to disinfect the ground with lime and burning, but the disease broke out again in the following summer and spread west of the Slave River and into the park. In spite of efforts to control it, it spread further into the park in 1964. It was found that men and machines working on the banks of the Slave River, in their summer range were causing the plains bison to drift westwards, towards the remaining wood bison herd.

Two dead animals, which it was suspected had died from anthrax, were found only a few miles from Needle Lake, so that the herd were in danger, not only from mixing with the hybrids, but from anthrax as well. The Needle Lake and Fort Smith corrals were still available and could be put in order. In 1965 another drive was held. Of the sixty-nine wood bison that could be located, forty-seven were captured. Forty of these were sent to the Fort Smith corral and twenty-three later transferred to the Elk Island Park, near Edmonton. In this beautiful park, they were quarantined in a large area but the herd was found to be still infected with tuberculosis and brucellosis. Over a period of years, all the adults had to be destroyed, leaving only the generations born in the park under the care of Chief Warden Bob Jones and his men.

The odyssey of the wood bison was not yet over. No sooner were they happily established and free from disease in the quarantine park (a lovely place of aspen woods, meadows, lakes, and sedge grass) than it was decided that the park was required for public use. The bison in the next two or three years would have to be moved to free range in their natural habitat.

It was as a result of this decision that Beryl and I came in a small way into the wood bison picture. Barry Gilbert, who was still at Edmonton, was involved with the future provincial game park. He was eager that we should have two wood bison calves as soon as possible after they were born in order that they, like the moose, might become imprinted by us, and would subsequently be easy to handle when transferred to the game park at Ministic.

The project was delayed for a year, but one morning in late May 1977, we found ourselves heading north in the Datsun to pick up our charges. The terms had been altered in that they were no longer destined ultimately for Ministic, but we were to raise the calves, to be joined later by a bull, so that we might have a small herd at the disposal of the Wildlife Service.

First we had to stop in Edmonton to sign various papers before the calves could be committed to our charge. Drake Hocking had made an appointment for us with the regional director for this purpose. While waiting for his arrival, we telephoned Elk Island and found to our dismay that the cows and calves had been released two days before, since they could not keep them penned indefinitely. Now they only had two bull calves in the pens. Having got the papers signed we decided to drive to Elk Island so that we might at least see a wood bison calf.

Elk Island Park is about forty miles east of Edmonton. We turned off the main road and crossed a cattle grid at the main gates. Then for several miles we drove through aspen woods and past shining lakes, the grass at their shorelines and along the side of the road brilliant in the afternoon sun. Presently, a large brown mound appeared at the side of the road, which turned into a shaggy plains bison that did not bother to lift its head as we passed. In the middle of all this loveliness were the park offices, set amongst well cared for green lawns. The Chief Warden, Bob Jones, had just left. He was called from the office on a small radio.

"No. I can't see them," his voice came booming back, "I'm on my way home. It's after four o'clock. See if you can get hold of Fred Dixon, he should be at the quarantine corrals."

"Say not the struggle nought availeth," I thought, as I remembered the 200 miles that we had to drive to get home, but there was a friend of a friend in the office, and he soon contacted Fred Dixon, who said that he would meet us at the park gates. He was already there when we arrived, and if he had been caught just before leaving for home himself, he didn't show it. He was a man of few words and had the small neat figure of a good horseman. He had been riding for the Parks Service for twenty years, much of this time with plains bison and wood bison, so that he spoke of them with impressive nonchalance when he spoke at all. He led us in his car across the main road to a padlocked gate, then along a dirt road between wire fences to another padlocked gate and so into the quarantine area. A mile further on we came to another gate in a high wire fence, which led to the corrals.

The wire fence was made of the same material as our own fence, heavy-duty nine gauge galvanized wire in six-inch squares, but this one was fastened to strong wooden posts, rather than the angle iron posts that we use. At the gate post, the wire had been torn away from the post and recently cobbled back into place. It looked as if a runaway lorry or a tank had hit it.

"What happened there?" I asked.

"Bull went through," replied Fred laconically.

"What on earth made him do that?" I asked, astounded that any animal, other than a rhino or an elephant, could burst such a fence.

"We didn't want him with the cows that we were bringing into the corral area, but he had other ideas. He went sort of mad after that and we couldn't do anything with him. Had to shoot him."

In the corrals there were several cows and two bull calves, one only two-days-old, and the other considerably older. We wanted cow calves, taken soon after birth, so these were no good for us, and anyway, they had not been separated from their cows.

"There'll be some more coming along," said Fred, "I'll be running them in after a day or two. Then we'll let you know and you can take your pick."

These cows were in a large holding corral, but the handling area was built like an old fortified trading post, with vertical logs forming an intricate pattern of pens, passages and chutes, with a walk-way along the tops of the walls, so that animals could be driven or guided from above and separated by the release of drop doors. The calves were much the same colour as a young moose, having a close, rather woolly, chestnut coat, a black nose, and large black eyes, ornamented by long lashes. After seeing them we looked forward all the more eagerly to getting our own but felt a little intimidated that a bull could go through a fence like ours if he wanted to. It wouldn't be for a few years at any rate, and perhaps then he would not have the desire.

About ten days later, we heard that some cows and calves had again been collected into the corrals and we set off once more, hotfoot for Elk Island Park. Fred Dixon, neat as ever, met us again at the gates.

"Had a hell of a job to find them," he told us, "but I've got three cow calves penned for you to see. A little older than you want them, but they were hiding from me."

We climbed up onto the walkway that led round the top of the stockades and were soon able to look down into the pen, where three small calves were moving anxiously round and round the walls. We chose the two smallest hoping that they were the youngest. The third calf looked too big to fit into the box that I had made.

"I'll just put a rope on them and bring them out," said Fred. "Will you back your truck up to the chute door?"

We let the tailboard down at the chute gate and stood on each side awaiting Fred's arrival with the first calf. Presently there was a noise of scuffling feet. We expected Fred to arrive first, dragging an unwilling calf on the end of a rope. Instead, the calf arrived first, dragging Fred. I had a brief glimpse of a chestnut calf, eyes staring, feet tucked up under its chin as it bounded at the end of a rope, like a greyhound at the end of a leash when a hare jumps up in front of it. Fred quickly got the rope off its neck and went back for the other, while Beryl and I blocked the first calf's escape. The second calf arrived in a similar fashion, and as soon as it was inside, I fastened the door and we roped the box down. There was a gap between the end of the box and the tailgate into which Beryl could squeeze, so that she might keep an eye on them. The sides of the box were shaking as the terrified calves pushed about and I wondered if the plywood was strong enough to hold them. I had left a gap of six inches between the top of the door and the top of the box, so that they could get some air.

"You'd better be off," said Fred, "and don't let them get their noses through that gap, or they'll be out on you."

The park road was rough, and the calves were fully occupied in keeping their balance, but once we were onto the smooth highway they discovered the gap above the door and started to try and force their way through. Beryl was kept busy pushing first one nose back and then the other, as they stamped about the floor in their efforts to escape. In the rear-view mirror, through a hole in the front of the box, I could see only their heaving backs. I stopped for a moment to see if Beryl was all right.

"Go on, go on," she cried and I set off again as if I was driving in the Indianapolis 500.

Presently I realized that the stamping had stopped and through the rear mirror I could see no heaving backs, but only, through the gap above the door, an expanse of highway. I felt certain that Beryl and the calves were lying strewn down the road a few miles back, but, on stopping again, found that all was well. The calves had collapsed and were lying down peaceably, while Beryl, looking a trifle wind-blown and exhausted, was preparing for another storm, lying wedged crossways in the back of the truck between the box and the tailgate.

"Do get on," she pleaded, "before it all starts again."

We must have set a record time for a small truck from Edmonton to Calgary and presently had the drive gates closed and knew that our calves were secure.

The shed that had been built for the swans, in their first winter, had now been designated as a calf house and filled with straw. We had made a small corral, using a corner of the game-park fence which lined the west side of the drive and completing the other two sides, which enclosed the shed, with a pole fence. It was not proposed that this should be a permanent enclosure, but we thought it strong enough and high enough to contain the calves. Beryl and I unloaded the first calf and pushed it inside without a struggle, and, forgetting as we often do, that increasing age brings few comforts and considerable physical deterioration, more marked in myself than in my wife, we turned confidently to unload the other. This one was eager to rejoin the first and to escape from us, so that it bounded with such force into my arms that I sat down on the ground, while Beryl fell on top of us in an attempt to hold it. We emerged from this football scrum still in possession of the ball. The calves began to pace backwards and forwards up and down the wire fence of the corral, dragging their heads against the fence as they turned in a pathetic and hopeless movement.

Although very small, they were far too quick and strong for Beryl and me to catch and for one to hold while the other fed with a bottle, at least until they realized the import of the bottle. Beryl telephoned John Stewart Smith, a neighbouring rancher, to ask for help. It is our great good luck to have as neighbours John and his wife, Avki, who are both from big farms in Tanzania which they had to give up owing to difficulties caused by the political situation. John came in the evening, bringing two young hands with him, Hamish Kerfoot, first over the fence in the balloon incident, and Ronnie Holmes, another neighbour's son. They caught the calves and held them while Beryl fed them from a bottle. John was surprised at their strength. He looked at us, his wide blue eyes, weathered by sun and sea, for he had been an officer in the Royal Navy as well as a farmer.

"You can't handle them like this," he said kindly. "They're far stronger than a calf at that age. I'll tell you what. We'll come round twice a day and hold them for you while you feed them." This promise was made in spite of the fact that he had about 300 cows of his own to look after and was still busy calving.

It was four days before we could manage the calves by ourselves. John thought the smallest calf to be three weeks to a month old, but it looked as if it had been held back by scours. The larger calf he guessed to be about two weeks old. The calves already showed different characteristics. The larger calf being the shyest, Beryl, with her gentler approach to animals, took as her own, while I adopted the smaller and tougher. Beryl called hers "Martha" and mine was named "Mary."

On the first morning, long before John and Hamish arrived for the feeding, I looked out of the window and saw only one calf in the corral. Martha was running up and down the fence inside, grunting anxiously. I hurried up the drive while Beryl stayed with Martha, and at the far end of the drive I discovered Mary at the gate. It was the closest she could get to Elk Island, 200 miles away, and I wondered if some instinct had made her head in that direction. As the bison got to know us, they became progressively more difficult to drive although they were often willing to follow. However, on this day they were still frightened of us and easy to drive. I drove Mary back to the pen, while Beryl hid inside the gate, ready to prevent Martha from coming out, and ready to shut the gate as soon as Mary was in. As Mary appeared Martha's grunts rose to a crescendo, and Mary hurried to the gate to join her.

Both calves were considerably older than they should have been for the purposes of successful imprinting. In time, they came to accept us in loco parentis, but not nearly as easily as they would have done had they been newly born. It just took much more time and trouble. Meanwhile they were the loneliest little orphans, missing their tousled cows, and our hearts went out to them as they paced up and down the fence rubbing the hair off their foreheads as they turned.

CHAPTER 11

Martha and Mary

HAND-REARED CALVES are usually fed only twice a day, when the time can be found to do it. Martha and Mary however, were special. We had badgered the Wildlife Service for two years, to give them to us, and now we wanted to bring them up under as favourable circumstances as possible. Also we didn't want the Parks people to be able to say, "I told you so!" if anything happened to confirm their opinion that we were not fit to have them.

To begin with, after the first four days, when we found that we could manage them by ourselves, we fed the calves four times a day. At the first feed, Beryl nearly lost the teat off the bottle down Mary's throat, so we had changed to a bucket, fitted with a rubber teat and ball valve, which made a "clink, clink, clink" sound, as the calf sucked. They were given evaporated milk and fresh cow's milk, mixed half and half and they never seemed to lose condition, even in the first day or two.

At first each calf had to be manoeuvered into a corner, Mary in the shed and Martha in the box that we used for training the moose calves before shipping. The object of getting the bison calves into the shed or box was that they would then associate going into a box with something nice, which would make them easier to handle if we had to confine them for some reason in the future. The teat had to be pushed at their noses and a little milk squirted onto their lips, before they would take hold. Mary learnt quickly but Martha had to have a finger inserted into her mouth, before the teat could be slipped inside. Mary seemed to be able to switch quickly from one step in her upbringing to the next, but not Martha. Once she had decided that the insertion of a finger in the corner of the mouth preceded the teat with a supply of warm milk, she insisted on having the finger before she would suck at the teat. I began to think that she was retarded, but Beryl declared that she was showing intelligence if not reasoning power. Anyway, she was two weeks younger than Mary.

During the first few days, when they were in the small pen, pacing up and down the fence, they rubbed the baby hair from their foreheads and the sides of their mouths as they turned. This quickly grew back in the dark hairs of their future coat and gave them a black forehead and a dark drooping line from the corners of their mouths, so that they had an ill-tempered and dissatisfied expression. We screened the pen with rolls of brown paper and wire, used in stucco building construction, and as soon as they could no longer see out their pacing stopped.

During the previous winter, before the calves came to us, Barry Gilbert, who was going to supervise the study of the calves, moved to another job. In his place we heard that Doctor Val Geist, our enthusiastic friend from the University of Alberta, was to be in charge. Val Geist came out to see us a day or two after the calves had arrived and was disappointed in their age.

"Far too late for successful imprinting," he told us as he looked at the nervous calves. "They should be following you everywhere." But presently, as is almost inevitable with Val, he brightened up.

"Now then," he said, "the first thing is to see that they recognize some place as home. A safe place, a place that they will come back to. Then we will extend their range gradually and see if they always come back to the same place. As they get older, we want to know when they feed and when they rest, what they eat, what grasses and shrubs they prefer. We want to know what their habits are, when they gambol and frisk, how they struggle for dominance. Just collect the type of grasses and wild flowers that they eat and send them to the university. We can identify them. I believe that no scientific study of this sort has been made of wood bison and I hope to get a grant so that I may put a student on to it. Ah, look. There is Mary. Or is it Martha? I shall never get them right. Let me see. Martha is the smallest, is she not?"

"Mary."

"Well it's Martha then. Now do you see? She is eating dirt. That perhaps is caused by some deficiency. Something that she is in need of. Well, I must be off, but I shall be back soon to see you."

As he rushed off to some other appointment, Beryl and I felt inundated by his enthusiasm and by all that he wanted us to observe. "I hope that we get the student soon," said Beryl, the one on whom most of the work was bound to fall.

Mary soon began to pluck at the grass inside the pen, but Martha was always a few days behind her in development. After about ten days we extended the corral, first by a hundred square yards, later by a thousand and after they had eaten the best of the grass in that, by another thousand. Then we extended their run to an acre between the drive fence and the fox runs. By this time, they had long ago given up their pacing and from the time the pen was first enlarged, it was no longer necessary to screen them from the world outside.

They were always fed in the original pen and Martha still had to be manoeuvered into a corner of the shed and have her mouth opened by a finger before the teat was pushed in. She was far more nervous than Mary, who was ready to be fed anywhere at any time. In order to get Martha into the shed we had to drive her, separating her from Mary who was now fed outside. If any pressure was put on Martha she would break back to rejoin Mary so that, as we quietly edged them both towards the shed, Beryl would say to Martha, "Now think, Martha, think." Martha would put on a puzzled and obstinate look, and it seemed she was really trying to think. Eventually she understood and preceded Beryl into the shed, but it was a slow process.

Beryl had been considering trying Atravet the drug she uses to calm the moose calves when training them for shipping, on Martha. She thought that if only she could soothe Martha sufficiently to take the teat without first having her mouth opened, we might avoid the necessity of driving her into the shed where she could be cornered.

Doctor Florence, the veterinarian of the Calgary Zoo, came out to see us. Beryl told him about her difficulties with Martha and asked his advice about Atravet.

"Atravet sometimes affects their coordination," he told her. "I should try a little Mellaril. It is very mild and actually not intended for veterinary use. I believe that it is commonly used for children who wet their beds."

Beryl, of course, was delighted with the whole idea, and gave Martha the pills in honey on the end of her fingers. In a very short time, Martha took the teat of her own accord. Thereafter, there was no more trouble, and they both fed outside. When Beryl told a doctor friend, a tall dour Scotsman, about her success, he said, "I've never heard of Mellaril being used for bed wetters. Mind you, it may be so. But I can tell you that it is a very fine anchor drug for schizophrenics."

Early one morning, when they were both hard at work on their milk buckets, the valves clanking rhythmically like small boat engines, Pollux appeared round the corner of the house. His horns were well grown but still in velvet, so that they looked clumsy on his head, like a statue still veiled. Discovering us feeding the bison, he came hopefully but shyly, since we rarely see him at this time, to the fence. The two bison calves, aware of movement behind them, let go of the teats in alarm. Then, seeing a large brown animal standing at the fence, a faulty recognition dawned, and with eager grunts they ran up to greet it. Alas, it was not a comforting bison cow, but someone tall and strange, who backed away in embarrassment and then moved off. Mary and Martha gazed after him, moved along the fence in an endeavour to keep near him, then stood disconsolate.

Before we got the bison we had heard that Tarjei Tennyson was doing a comparative study on the reaction of wild and domestic animals to human handling, at the University Experimental Farm, Edmonton. He had two plains-bison calves, two yak calves, and two Hereford calves in his care. We arranged to meet him at the farm and found that he looked rather like Lord Tennyson as a young man, although he protested that he had no connection with the poet and that his parents came from Norway. He had a very easy, relaxed manner with his animals, and they responded in a similar way.

"Are those buffalo chips?" asked Beryl, looking at some dry droppings and thinking of the fires that the old plainsmen used to make from them. "Is that what they should look like? Not like cow pats?"

"Yes," he replied. "In fact, if they were to get moister than that, I should begin to get worried and think that something was wrong."

Beryl has always had a certain respect for the opinions of some experts, although by no means all. While we were sailing, Eric Hiscock had been the authority, and she could have picked no better, although I sometimes got tired of hearing him quoted. Now Tarjei Tennyson became her expert on bison droppings and his lightly expressed opinion was to lead us on a great dance.

We normally get milk once a week from another farm neighbour, Edna Iredale, but since the arrival of the bison she had been able to provide a gallon of milk every day. She had a quota to fill, and it wasn't easy, but she has the softest of hearts. "Oh, the poor wee things," she cried when I told her of how they had thought that Pollux was their mother, "they must need the milk. I can manage for another day or two."

While they had so much cow's milk their droppings seemed all right, but the day came when we had to put them on a substitute. It may have been the substitute, or it may have been that they were now eating more grass, but their droppings became very loose. Not actually scouring, but loose enough to cause Beryl anxiety.

"I expect that it's only the change in their diet," I told her.

"Well you know what Tarjei Tennyson said," she replied. "He said that if the droppings weren't 'chips' he'd think something was very wrong."

With continual harping on what Tarjei Tennyson said, I began to get worried myself. Twice a day I carefully cleaned up their droppings, as assiduously as any Indian "sweeper" had ever done in the Indian cavalry lines when I was a soldier long ago. Anything faintly resembling a chip was greeted with delight, any trace of diarrhea, with dismay. We bought bottle after bottle of Kaopectate. Whereas a spoonful or two had always cured the moose calves, the bison seemed to lap it up without any noticeable effect. Doctor Florence suggested yogurt mixed with their milk. When this proved unsatisfactory we tried various medicines recommended by our rancher friends. Eventually, Bruce Gilbert, whose ranch lands extend to the north and south of our place, suggested that it might be the milk substitute that was upsetting them. "Susan gives our kids Meadowlands powdered milk, and they do fine on that. Why don't you give it a go?" We switched to Meadowlands powdered milk, which is a pure hydrated milk and bought it by the case. Meanwhile, John Quine suggested that we should mix a saline solution with their milk. This and the Meadowlands powdered milk proved to be the answer, and Beryl was soon satisfied. Perhaps, after all, the change in diet and the green grass were all that was wrong with them.

The calves were now beginning to change colour from light chestnut to dark brown, so dark that it could almost be described as black. Their horns were growing and they were beginning to look more bulky about the shoulders. They often played together, butting and pushing each other and making short dashes through the aspen trunks. Sometimes they would prop on all four legs together, or whirl about on the forehand, the axis on which they preferred to spin. It was soon necessary to look out for these whirling quarters lest we should be sent flying ourselves. When their run was increased to an acre we began to call them by tilting the bucket so that the valve was free of milk. Then working the valve, we found that the clinking soon brought them to us. Later, when they were given the whole drive to run in, we called them by name while clanking the handle of the bucket.

Although their hearing was good, their reactions were exasperatingly slow. Gradually, the distant clinking would impinge on their dim little minds, and they would look towards the sound and lick their lips. Then they would take a few steps towards us and stop to pick a blue aster, a dandelion or a buttercup head. The heads of flowers were their favourite browse, particularly that of the purple vetch. Their movements were so leisurely to start with, the interests so numerous that distracted them, that they might take twenty minutes to get to the house.

In order to encourage their progress, one of us would leave a bucket of milk with the other and walk up the drive to meet them. We avoided trying to drive them, but rather walked with them, because we wanted them to feel that the house was the centre of their territory, that it was the place from which good things emanated, and that they were going there on their own accord. As they got nearer to the house their pace would quicken and suddenly up would go their tails, and they'd make a mad dash for the milk. Beryl and I were both jealous of our own calves and liked to feed each one ourselves so that when this dash started we too had to dash or hobble as well as we could in order to recover the extra bucket, before the holder of both was upset by the eagerness of the two calves, and, of course, lest the affection of one's own calf should be won away. The calves had very soon recognized their own person, and Mary would come to me, Martha to Beryl.

June and July are months of thunder and rain, rain which causes the grass to grow as quickly as do Pollux's horns. Halfway through July, the farmer relies on a dry spell to get the hay cut and baled. Then he eyes with suspicion the dark clouds that circle overhead, as the lightning flickers between them and splits the blackness.

That year was relatively dry, but the one thunderstorm that hit us was exceptional. In the afternoon, the clouds had been building up into towering thunderheads, until in the evening the whole of the western sky was black, with a ragged hem of cloud hanging low over the mountains. Only in one small place was the setting sun breaking through the blackness, illuminating a hole in the clouds, whose edges glowed redly, so that the whole western sky looked like some great inverted volcano, with red hot lava pouring from the crater. On each flank of the approaching storm, brilliant snakes' tongues of lightning flickered repeatedly to the ground, and every minute of its ominous and slow approach, the rumble of the thunder grew louder.

The storm passed over us, the worst of it hitting to the North. The wind arrived with a sudden rush that ripped the forgotten washing from the line while the rain cascaded down. The aspens paled before the onslaught as the wind buffeted them and exposed the undersides of the leaves. The grass in the hayfields scurried and cringed, while, further afield, the tall green oats and the barley seemed to wave to the clouds, as if pleading to be spared from an attack by hail.

I wanted to see what reaction the bison calves had to this turmoil and put on oilskins and rubber boots to go out. We had our two grandchildren staying with us, aged eight and nine. I met them in the hallway outside their bedroom, from where they had been watching the lightning.

"We're frightened, Grandpa," they said.

"How disgusting. What on earth are you frightened for?" I asked.

"Because of the lightning. Aren't you frightened?"

"No. Of course not. Anyway I have my gum boots on."

"What difference does that make?"

"Rubber's a good insulator, so the lightning won't hit me."

I went outside and had only gone a short distance when there was the most stupendous explosion above me, as if I had been standing beside a fifteen-inch gun when it fired. Simultaneously a bolt of lightning struck the transformer on its pole a few yards from the house. I found myself cowering near the ground. "So much for saying you are not afraid," I thought. When I discovered the bison calves they were completely unperturbed, lying together on the wet earth, their eyes half closed, quietly chewing the cud as the rain poured off their backs and ran in rivulets around them. They seem to be similarly unmoved by hail, whereas Petruska and her calf, some years before, had panicked during her first real hailstorm.

I telephoned Calgary Power about the transformer, the electricity now being off. At two in the morning, three cheerful and enthusiastic young men arrived and rigged a tackle, lowered the old transformer, and hoisted a new one into place. Since the transformer pole was in a fox pen, only the one who climbed the pole went into the pen, in order not to disturb the foxes. The heavy transformer was hoisted from outside the pen, which to a certain extent added to their difficulties. Those young men were just the people for a rough night at sea in a small yacht when things start to go wrong.

Next morning Beryl found the grandchildren in bed, sleeping happily and wearing their gum boots.

By August the bison were a uniform dark brown, the hair on their foreheads being quite black. They suffered from the heat and lay down for most of the day. However, if we were doing anything round the house or in the drive they always appeared — to help us we used to say, although, of course, they simply liked companionship and were always curious. One day we were laying stones along that part of the game-park fence which borders the road, in order to prevent the foxes from escaping. The bison had followed us through a gap we had made in the snow fence which had been put up to keep them away from the road fence. They had never been so close to the road before. We had forgotten about the bison and they had wandered away again for about fifty yards when a truck roared past throwing up a cloud of dust. It was the bison's first experience with close fast-moving traffic. Up went their tails and they galloped full pelt, not into the safety of the woods, but back to us. We felt that we had finally been accepted and that they had come to us, we hoped, for protection.

After we had finished laying the stones and driven the Landrover back through the gap in the fence, the bison followed us in their companionable way, and we were able to close it behind them. However, they did not forget about whatever they had seen or found between the snow fence and the road fence, and a day or two later we saw them near the road fence and found that they had jumped the snow fence and what they hadn't jumped they'd broken down. We were not worried about them because the cattle that use the road had gone long ago to the forest reserve and would not be back along it until October, so there was no chance of infection, nor did we think that they would continue to go there as soon as their interest for something new had abated.

Our neighbouring ranchers are always interested in the growth of our moose calves and were naturally even more interested in bison calves which resemble their cattle. It wasn't long before the Larsens, two sisters who run an efficient operation to the north of our place, rang up to say that they had been watching the calves at the gate.

"How old are they?" Lil Larsen asked.

"Three months," I replied, proud as a new father.

"Well they appear to be doing very well. But one thing," she continued, "if you don't mind my saying so, they seem to be breathing very hard. I thought I'd tell you, because if we had a calf breathing like that, we'd think that he was sick for sure."

"They just start puffing the minute the sun comes out," I told her. "They are eating very well but I think that their coats are too woolly, and they are a bit dim about finding shade."

For a few days we watched them anxiously but the moment the sun went down, they stopped puffing. We decided that bison just suffer in hot weather. Later, in winter we were to discover that no matter what the wind, nor how cold it might be, whereas the moose would choose a sunny spot to sit in, the bison cared not a damn and were perfectly happy in the shade.

CHAPTER 12

Martha and Mary: Growing Up

SEPTEMBER CAME all too quickly. Early one morning, the clover, still green and fresh, was nipped by the frost, and there was a chill in the air which brought with it a feeling of exhilaration, an exhilaration which sent the bison galloping through the trees, and Hardy, the moose calf, striking at the bushes with his forefeet. Pollux, Petruska, and Hardy all came to the house together, as if the two older moose had been reminded of their winter routine by the nip in the air. Pollux's horns, with the velvet newly rubbed off, were white and shining, and he stalked up full of a new pride.

From time to time since their first meeting, the bison and the moose had seen each other through the fence. Pollux and Hardy disregarded the bison, but Petruska was jealous of Beryl's interest. If the bison were near the fence, she came stalking along it on the other side, with her ears back as if she was going to strike at them through the fence. She never did so, nor did the bison show any fear. We wondered what would happen at the end of the first year, when the double fence was completed and we could put them into the reserve together.

Martha and Mary were still being fed a mixture of powdered milk and evaporated milk. We intended to continue to feed them, as their cows would have done, until the end of the winter, and the snow was gone. They were also being fed a small amount of calf starter pellets and beet pulp at midday. They were given the milk but for the calf starter pellets, which they were given in the drive, we made them come up to us, rather than putting their feed in front of them.

They spent their time equally either in the aspen trees near the house or in the drive, but they seemed to prefer the sown grasses and the clover on the edge of the drive, rather than the wild grasses in the trees. However, they were fairly promiscuous feeders, plucking a leaf here and a leaf there from the willows and young aspen and more rarely pulling at the ends of a spruce bough or sampling the scrub birch. We never saw them eating the sedge grass in the dry ponds, which we had heard bison liked. Perhaps there was plenty of better-tasting food available.

By the end of September, the aspen had all turned, and the country was clothed in its autumn colours, the brown of the grasslands, the gold of the aspen, and the dark green of the spruce trees. The mountains that for the past three months had appeared either light gray or blue above the tree line (according to the weather and the time of day) now had their outline softened by the snow on their upper slopes. The hay was stacked in the fields, and the cattle due to return from their summer pastures.

The bison, in their new dark coats, now began to look heavy about the shoulders. They carried their heads low, as if bent in meditation and were very strong and short between knee and fetlock, with chaps of long black hair behind the forearm. They had butting and pushing matches several times a day. Mary was the aggressor, but Martha was the biggest (although in my eyes not the cleverest) and usually came out best. When Mary came up for her feed, she came tossing her shaggy head in the most engaging way, as if throwing the hair away from her eyes. Sometimes she advanced towards us, when we had no feed in our hands, in the same manner. She was then, in fact, offering a challenge, or a request to play, which amounted to the same thing and had to be discouraged. A nudge from a bison, even only five-months-old is no weak prod.

When the snow came and hid the grass in the drive, we put a hayrack in the training box and fed the bisons a little hay each day. In order to get at it, one of them had to go into the box, while the other fed at the other end of the box. This was to train them so that they could be boxed or confined without panic, but ever since they had had their first milk in the shed, they had had no inhibitions about going into confined places. We kept the hay in a small shed, and if by any chance the door was not properly closed, they loved to get inside. Mary, in particular, liked to climb up on the hay bales.

They did this not because they were hungry or in need of shelter, but because they enjoyed knocking the hay bales down, breaking the twine with their horns, and being surrounded by such a wealth of hay. They never stayed in long.

We had some very cold weather before Christmas and a good snowfall which promised to improve the water level when the run-off came in the spring. As we wanted the bison to learn about foraging in the snow, they were given, except when they got into the hay shed, about five pounds of hay a day, a much reduced ration of milk, and two or three pounds of calf starter pellets. They thrived on this, but made a gesture of looking for food on their own by wiping the snow away with their noses and foreheads and plucking some dead grass. Small green shoots could sometimes be seen amongst the dead stems, and these they pulled out with the help of their black, pointed, prehensile tongues.

They spent much of their time round the house, where we usually found them resting under the overhanging eaves at its western end. One of the disadvantages of their always being near was the number of droppings that I had to collect in order to preserve the snow's original whiteness. Fortunately these steaming offerings were almost immediately frozen hard and could be piled like cow dung to be carried away to other people's gardens.

There was no doubt that the bison were getting enough to eat, but they were so often stretched out full length in the snow, or lying contentedly chewing the cud, impervious to the ferocity of the wind or weather, that Beryl and I began to wonder whether they were getting enough exercise. We, therefore, walked or skied every day to the end of the drive carrying their ration of pellets in two plastic bowls. As we passed them, we called them, "Martha, Mary. Come and get your feed."

Generally they continued to sit there, chewing away, like two fat, black-clad people on a park bench, chewing peanuts and watching the world go by.

"Martha, Mary," we called, as we started up the drive, and then, our shoulders bent against the north wind, we shuffled up towards the far gate.

Sometimes Martha or Mary would stretch out one black foreleg as we passed, but in general their attitude was that it was simply not worth getting up for so small a ration. Halfway up the drive we'd stop and call again. As long as they saw us, Martha and Mary lay still, thinking perhaps that there was a chance that we would return, but now that we were out of sight their interest was aroused, and perhaps their anxiety. First one would get up and stretch and then the other, and then slowly, slowly, as if every step was painful, one followed the other through the trees, until they both disappeared to one side. "Martha, Mary. What on earth are you doing," was our usual cry.

Suddenly, out of the trees they'd come, at full gallop, the deep and powdery snow flying out at each side, as if they were two small snow ploughs. The depth of snow seemed to hinder them less than it may have hindered the cannon balls, which they sometimes resembled.

The door of the downstairs living room is a stable door, made in two halves, with a wooden latch on the inside, and it is opened from the outside by pulling a thong which passes through a hole in the door. The wooden latch does not necessarily fall into place, and the door fits tightly, making it easy to forget to check that the latch is down. The bison soon learned that if they pushed the door it might open, and if it opened they came inside.

The upstairs living room is where Beryl and I spend most of our time when in the house. Through its dormer windows and through the big west window there is a wonderful view of the mountains and the game park, but because of the overhanging roof we cannot see who may be at the door. Our first warning of an intrusion was usually the sound of a slow and careful tread on the floor downstairs. The first time that this happened Beryl called, "Hallo. Who's that? We're here. Come upstairs." A gusty sigh was the only answer to this invitation, and on going to the top of the stairs to welcome our visitors we found that they were the two bison.

One day they came in with their feet iced up. Instead of the sound of the slow tread there was a strange clatter. They found movement difficult. Martha was always the most nervous, the most guilt-ridden, and when we ordered them out, her feet shot from under her, and she fell on the floor. She caught her chin on a wooden bench which saved her from going flat down. Then she used it as a lever to get on her knees again. Otherwise, I really do not know how we would have got her to her feet. She was near the door and was able to get out, but in order to ensure Mary's safe withdrawal on her icy feet, we had to move a carpet so that she could walk on it in safety. As a result of Martha's spill, it was nearly a year before she ventured into the house again. But Mary, for whom Martha was the door opener, was a constant visitor. It was usually sufficient to shout down to her, "Mary. Out. Out you go," for her to turn round and make for the outside, but the door was as far as she got for Martha would be standing in the door in order to watch Mary's progress. Apart from muddy footprints if it was wet, she never made a mess and only on rare occasions upset anything such as a wastepaper basket or a small table.

On the whole they respected the fences, but one day, when they had got into the fox runs through an open gate and after I had enticed Mary out, Martha took a short cut from inside in order to join her. In doing this she walked straight through a rabbit wire fence, stretched on a seven-foot steel frame. She did it like a lion in a circus, jumping through a paper hoop.

It was a cold winter with the snow lying deep and powdery over the countryside. The bison in their black coats stood out against the bright snow, taking their place as naturally as the moose in the winter colour scheme, amongst the light gray trunks of the aspen with their black scars, the black shadows on the snow, and the dark spruce trees. The busy chickadees were back at the fat hung on the two spruce trees in front of the house, which they shared with the downy and hairy woodpeckers.

One night there was a telephone call to ask if our moose were out. The speaker, driving down the road past the drive gates, had seen a cow moose and a calf in his headlights. Although we frequently get this sort of call, since there are moose in the vicinity, we usually check to ensure that the gates are shut and that the fence has not been drifted up so that the moose could get out. Petruska had already been to the house with her calf that evening so we were not worried about this possibility. We went to have a look, nevertheless, and found the gate shut. Outside, we picked up the track of a moose between the road and the fence. It appeared to be by itself, and we saw that it had not turned down the road allowance but had gone on into the other part of the farm. We thought no more about it.

Six weeks later, Beryl was looking out of the kitchen window, having just fed Petruska, Pollux, and Hardy, when I heard her say,

"My God, there are four." Through the door I saw a fourth moose, a cow by the look of her, although it is not always so easy to tell when the horns are gone. She was on the other side of the willows in front of the house, moving timidly past, as if she knew that the others were getting something good to eat, but did not dare to approach closer. She was a fine-looking moose, in good condition, a little bigger than Petruska. Although she was there in front of our eyes, we could not fully believe what we saw. The fence was seven feet high all round the game park, and although this was reduced in places by a foot or a foot and a half of snow, we had never imagined anything jumping in.

Petruska was at the salt when she saw the intruder. She put her ears back and stalked towards her in a threatening manner. She was closely followed by Hardy, also with his ears back and his ruff up. Pollux, who was still at the feed bowls, looked on like me, in mild surprise and disbelief. Beryl, on the other hand, hurried out to support her darling in case of a fight. Of course, our moose must have known about the "Wild One" as she came to be called. Very little goes on in the game park that they do not know about. What had upset Petruska and caused Pollux's mild surprise was her arrival at the house, which they regard as their special preserve. And the one vice that burns deep in Petruska's otherwise gentle heart is jealousy. Whether it was Petruska's menacing advance or the appearance of Beryl at the door, I cannot say, but the Wild One turned away and trotted off. Petruska stopped and watched her go and since she was retreating, Hardy took the lead and followed her, ears back, for a short way.

Now that we had a new moose inside I remembered the telephone call of a few weeks before and of the fact that we had only seen the tracks of one moose. I also remembered that about the same time I had noticed the top of the fence near the gate being slightly bent inwards. The fence was such an obstacle that I still had not considered the possibility of a moose jumping in there, especially as the take-off from the road ditch would be from slightly lower ground. We went to examine the fence again. The top had been bent inwards for about one and a half feet at an angle of forty degrees and the single strand of barbed wire at the inside and top of the fence, which is stretched between short iron arms fastened to the top of the fence posts and adds another ten inches to the height of the fence, had been pulled down and was caught in the angle between the arm and the top of the post. There was no trace of hair on the barbed wire, and the footprints had been buried in new snow, but this was the only place where there was any sign of bending of the fence. We had to assume that she had been frightened by the arrival of a car and had successfully tackled the fence, while the calf, whose tracks we had seen, ran along the fence outside.

"How on earth are we going to get rid of her?" Beryl asked in exasperation.

"I don't know," I said, "but I'm sure there'll be an opportunity."

"Anyway, I'm not going to have her in the game park," said Beryl with determination. "I'm sure that Petruska will be unhappy, and anyway we just can't have more moose. I suppose that she will have been bred and will have a calf, and how the hell am I going to tell which is Petruska, and which is the wild one when I want to handle the calf. I'm going to ring up the Wildlife Service and get them to do something about it."

"I don't expect that we can do anything till the snow has gone, because even if we get someone to tranquilize her, we'll have to get her out. By the time the snow has gone she will be getting near calving time and it will be too late."

"Well I'm going to ring them up anyway."

This she did and the problem was passed from one office to another until it finally arrived at Cochrane. "We'll just have to play it by ear," said the Fish and Wildlife Service there, which meant that if we had let a wild moose into the game park, it was up to us to get it out. They were not prepared to do anything about it, unless we told them that we had it in a truck, and then they would give us permission to move it.

About this time, we had news that the government was prepared to make a grant towards the behavioural study of our wood bison, and this study was to be carried out by a student from the Department of Environmental Design of Calgary University under the direction of Doctor Val Geist, the expert on ungulates.

It is his contention that past experience with the transplant of unconditioned bison has shown that they tend to disperse and wander away from the intended new home range, leading to conflicts with other land uses in that area. There is also considerable evidence to show that social ungulates, such as mountain sheep, caribou, and bison learn home ranges from their parents rather than by their own exploring.

The alternatives to transferring large groups of unconditioned bison to a selected range is to transfer a small group of semi-domesticated bison to the range, together with their handlers and to continue their handling and feeding until they have accepted the new location as their home range. They would then be unlikely to quit the selected range. Starting with these animals, the herd could then be built up gradually. Martha and Mary, already imprinted on human handlers, although perhaps not as much as Val Geist would have liked, offered the opportunity to study the timing and the rate of their exploration, when released to the game park from the drive. However, before this could be effected, we had to build our double fence, a condition laid down by the Wood Bison Committee.

Martha and Mary had first been penned in a corner of the fence which enclosed the drive. Later, when released in the drive, their movement had been controlled by the same fence, particularly the type to which they were accustomed. Since the time when we had first put up these fences, the cost of fencing had doubled, as had the cost of labour. In order to keep the cost within bounds, or at least the bounds within which the government was prepared to give financial assistance, we decided on a five-foot fence of six-inch squared galvanized heavy-duty wire, with iron posts driven every ten feet. We would do all the work ourselves, with such help as we could muster on the weekends.

Although the board set up by the Wood Bison Committee to inspect our place had laid down the condition that the whole game park should be double fenced, we had protested that to double the fence along the road and along the road allowance was a needless waste of money, since both the road and the road allowance were only used twice a year, when cattle were driven to and from their summer pasture. At these times, it is easy for us to control the bison by putting them in the drive where they are double fenced anyway, but it is also most unlikely that they would penetrate the woods as far as the road fences, except in winter when their search for forage may send them further afield. In winter there are no cattle moving along the roads, nor are there any in the fields adjoining the game park. In summer there are cattle pastured in the fields adjoining the game park to the south and west, and here we had to put up a double fence to prevent the bison from making any contact with the cattle, in whom, however, they seem to be entirely disinterested.

Most of the work was done on weekends, when there was no lack of helpers, far younger than ourselves. They seemed to enjoy a day of hard work in the country, or perhaps in their kindness they thought that we would never be able to complete it by ourselves, and instead might one day be found, feet up in a swamp, buried under a roll of wire. We were also lucky that the student, George Kollin, had arrived and commenced his study of the bison.

Bison George, as he came to be known, had left Hungary in a rucksack on his father's back in 1956. He had come to Calgary from McGill University in Montreal and was working in the Department of Environmental Design under Val Geist. He was slightly built, dark eyed, black haired, and wore a beard. I imagine that he had had little previous experience either of country life or of animals. We soon had him at work on the fence, which we felt was an integral part of his studies. "Recognition by wood bison of control exerted by a five-foot fence" could be a paragraph in his thesis on wood bison, if ever he wrote one. To begin with, Bison George stayed with us in the house and took over the feeding of the bison. He got on well with gentle Martha, but Mary he regarded with suspicion and perhaps a little nervousness. Mary, like all animals, recognized this immediately and sometimes walked after him, hoping for more feed and tossing her head in insistence. Bison George's voice, protesting, "No Mary. Mary. Mary, no," a litany of no great confidence, is one of the sounds that I associate with this period.

Bison George took his studies most seriously and the drive was soon marked out by four foot stakes into numerous small areas, so that he could note where the bison were at any time of day or night, and what they were doing. The tops of the stakes he carefully painted blue. He was then ready to commence his observation of the bison on the lines that Val Geist had laid down. On the first day he set off, wearing a peaked cap and a wind-proof jacket, his field glasses and camera round his neck, a clipboard and notebook in one hand, his pencil poised in the other, a look of eager concentration and anticipation on his face. A young biologist in the field. He was back a few hours later.

"I simply can't stand it," he cried. "I have watched them for four hours, and they have just lain down and done absolutely nothing except ruminate. They haven't moved."

Possibly with the help of a novel in his pocket, Bison George managed to adjust to the bisons' tempo. He religiously followed their every move. If they were standing, somewhere near, also standing, would be their shadow. If they were sitting, Bison George would also be sitting as well, either brooding on the placidity of bison or reading a novel. Later he stooped so far as to take a collapsible chair with him.

Bison George found the observation of the bison at night more difficult, since they were then nervous and tended to move away from him as soon as he got near. I do not know what his conclusions were about their behaviour at night, but from my own observation it is difficult to establish any definite pattern. In fact, I think that there is no particular pattern other than that they alternate grazing with ruminating and resting. The length of time spent in each operation depends on the weather, the amount of forage available, and how hungry they are. In hot weather, by day they were usually resting from about ten in the morning until four in the afternoon, and sometimes for an even longer time. This is the only period that I could count on for a more or less standard behaviour, although it was often broken by short periods of grazing. When a computer spews out the result of Bison George's observations, and I am proven wrong, I shall accept the computer's opinion — with qualifications.

Bison George intended to follow the movement of the bison, with the aid of radio tracking collars. In order to prepare them for wearing a collar, we started putting a rope or a strap round their necks. They offered no resistance nor did they seem to be conscious of wearing this neck gear.

When the bison were some distance away, Beryl and I, who might be compared to the parents of identical twins, had difficulty in differentiating between them. If they were close together we could tell by the difference in size, as Martha was still a little bigger. At close range they were easy to tell apart. Martha had a broader muzzle and a gentler expression, and there were other minor differences but they were only apparent to people who had been constantly with them. Bison George had no hope of telling them apart. I tied a blue ribbon on one of Mary's horns to help him. When she rubbed this off I suggested that I should paint one of her horns blue. Bison George was so shocked at this suggestion that I felt quite embarrassed at having made it. Instead we tied a yellow rope around Martha's neck.

Martha and Mary were both adept at opening the gates into the fox pens and loved to go inside and graze on the well-fertilized grass. We would have been happy to leave them in, in order to keep the grass down, but they also enjoyed pushing over the fox kennels or demolishing the woodpile under which Napoleon had his earth. They also viewed our attempts to drive them out as a game in which they were always victorious. The only way to get them out was to wait until they wanted to get out themselves and then to open the gate for them. We eventually had to fix the latches so that they could not raise them with their muzzles.

The mile of double fencing was completed within a year of the bison's arrival, and Val Geist arrived to witness Mary and Martha's release into the park. A month previously, I had left the gate unlatched, and Mary had pushed it open and entered the reserve. Almost immediately her tail had gone up into the question mark that indicates a bison's excitement, and she had dashed hither and thither, whirling on her forehand as she turned, delighted at the extension of her territory. I had shut the gate before Martha followed her, and Martha stood, grunting with anxiety, while she watched Mary cavorting on the other side of the fence. After Mary had tired of her galloping, and since no one had tried to drive her back, she returned on her own accord. Now that we were about to open the gate again, we expected some sort of similar performance.

Neither attempted to leave the drive. If they had opened the gate themselves, it would have been a different story. Eventually I had to go through first and call Mary, and when they finally came through, the excitement did not compare to Mary's first entry.

"Now you will see that they will explore their new territory," said Val, "and then they will come back to reassure themselves."

This is exactly what they did. They went perhaps fifty yards along the front of the house, then up went their tails and back they came—not to us, but to our vicinity, as they did not want to be put back through the gate. They went north as far as the trees, chose not to enter them, came back to the fence and checked that the drive was still there. Presently they started grazing, but at no time had they gone more than two hundred yards from the place that they knew. This was all in accordance with Val's theory that they would consider the house and the drive their home ground, a place to which they would always return.

In the next few days, they extended their exploration, and Bison George tramped after them. One morning he burst into the house after breakfast. "They are away up in the corner to the north," he said, pointing to the east, "but I saw the moose and thought that I had better quit. I've been up since three o'clock." It was obvious that to be up early in the morning, to follow the bison, to see the sun rise, and to meet a moose, was an adventure for Bison George, and I regretted the decline of my own enthusiasms. It might have been even more of an adventure if Petruska had gone after him, as there is no telling what her reactions will be when she has a calf with her.

Beryl and I get up early but like to recover some of the rest that we have lost by a short period of leisure after lunch. One day, at this sacred time, George again burst into the house. "Beryl, Beryl," he called. "Come quickly. There's something wrong with Mary. She's hyperventilated and hyperinflated."

"What the hell does he mean?" I grumbled as we hurried down the stairs. Martha and Mary were lying under their favourite tree behind the house. Mary was lying stretched out and puffing, and in this position did look a little blown up, but it was nothing unusual. "They were down by the pond and couldn't see the house," Bison George explained. "Then they panicked and stampeded up here."

"Perhaps they were bothered by those big horseflies," Beryl suggested. "They make the cattle run. No wonder they are puffing now after galloping all that way, on full stomachs too, I suppose."

"Yes," Bison George admitted ruefully, but with some relief. "They'd been grazing for about three hours."

Once the bison had completed the survey of their domain, they remained always in the open ground, a triangle stretching south between the house and the pond and covering about a third of the game farm. Bison George told us that during this initial exploration they appeared nervous and never ate much nor rested until they were back near the house or at least had the house in sight. Now they can usually be seen from the upstairs windows and only occasionally go into the shade of the aspens behind the fox pens.

They prefer the open ground, which is covered by scrub birch and natural grasses, willow and isolated spruce trees. They spend part of their grazing time up to their knees at the edge of the pond, pulling at the grass and willows that grow there.

The radio collars that Martha and Mary wore during the early days had not been of much assistance. The small transistors were sewn into a broad leather strap which buckled round their necks. Owing to the shape of a bison's neck, it had been impossible to keep the transmitter at the top of the collar without it slipping round. The transmitters were, therefore, at the bottom of the collar, under the neck, where the short whip aerial was vulnerable. Martha's aerial broke off, but Mary wore hers for a couple of weeks and appeared to experience no inconvenience.

The design and the protection of the transmitters was excellent, but this standard collapsed completely when it came to the direction finder on the receiving end. This resembled a TV aerial on a pole, which Bison George carried about with him, like Neptune with his trident, who had unhappily found himself ashore. The reception came with equal strength from every direction, as if the receiver was in the centre of a transmitter-equipped bison herd. On the morning that George met the moose, the awkward equipment was wisely abandoned and never used again. Nor was it necessary, for a glance out of the window by day was enough to discover the bison. At night an efficient direction finder could have been helpful, but the bison usually started their nightly peregrinations from the vicinity of the house and George, if he were so inclined, could follow them from there.

CHAPTER 13

Up and Down with the Foxes

KEEPING TRACK of our foxes' careers is as difficult as placing all the characters in *Henry Esmond.* After Louis and Louisa were gone, we were left with our two original pairs, Nelson and Emma, Napoleon and Josephine, and Emma's two cubs known as Bold Baby and Shy Baby.

In order to prevent the squabbles and the stealing of cubs that had marred their relations of the previous years, we separated Napoleon and Josephine from Nelson and Emma by dividing the big run, and we built another run of about fifteen hundred square yards for Shy Baby and Bold Baby. When the breeding time came, the night-long barking and fighting, Napoleon's one aim seemed to be to get through the fence to Emma, and Nelson's to reach Josephine. In Bold Baby's run we did not often see the vixen, who spent most of the day in the kennel, under which she was busily digging an earth.

One evening Bruce Gilbert rang up to say that he had seen a swift fox at the corner of the road, a mile from the house. For a moment we thought that it might be the long lost Louis, but then discovered that Josephine was missing. Next morning she was back in the same pen as Nelson and Emma. Josephine and Nelson seemed contented to be together again and so we allowed the vixens to change their mates, Emma going to Napoleon and Josephine to Nelson, thinking that if the vixens had already been bred, the dogs could function perfectly well as foster fathers. If they hadn't been bred, we thought that they would now have a chance with the dogs that they seemed to prefer. As a result of this unhappy decision, neither pair had any cubs. Meanwhile, Shy and Bold Baby had been busy in secret and one day, against all predictions and to our complete surprise, produced two beautiful cubs. During succeeding nights they dug through under the fence to join Napoleon and Josephine, and Josephine took over the surveillance of the family group. The cubs were called Taffy and Tony.

After being with these little foxes for several years, we can say with assurance, that some swift foxes can climb like cats, and others don't climb at all, but are confirmed diggers and gnawers. The diggers and gnawers can be stopped from escaping by buried wire netting, but a dedicated climber is difficult to control. Josephine, having taken on a certain responsibility for the new cubs, was determined to see that they were properly fed. In this pursuit I saw her climb the seven-foot fence at the back of the run, negotiate the overhang that we thought was fox proof, and then sit on top of it. From this elevation she quietly surveyed the countryside. She then jumped down, alighting as gently as a falling leaf, and bounded away with that exquisite swift fox gait. They seem to float rather than to run, and their feet barely touch the ground.

Several times we saw her return from these expeditions by another route, with a vole or a mouse in her mouth for Shy Baby's cubs. At one point, a five-foot rail fence joins the fox-run fence at right angles. Josephine jumped onto the lower rail, then onto the middle rail, and then on to the upper rail, with the ease and nonchalance of someone who daily mounts a short flight of steps. Then she ran along the top rail and jumped down into the pen where she started clucking to call the cubs to the feast. She became so confident in her hunting that one day, before the snow came, she disappeared altogether, and we feared that she had been killed by a coyote or a great horned owl, run over on the road, or poisoned. Napoleon was now a widower — it turned out later that he was a grass widower — and lived in the drive underneath a woodpile. He always came out when visitors arrived and we called him our P.R. Fox.

In order to allow our foxes a chance to prepare for their eventual release to the wild, we had fox proofed the whole of the drive area, first by putting rabbit wire along the game-park fences which enclosed it, then by burying a horizontal strip along the bottom and hanging a loose strip along the top, so that a climbing fox would find himself between the fence and the overhang. This was successful as far as the climbers were concerned, but we found that the diggers and gnawers could break a strand of rabbit wire, and one broken strand would let them through. We therefore laid fieldstones all along the bottom of the fence on top of the buried wire and fastened an additional four-foot strip of tougher welded netting along the fence above the stones. We were now confident that the foxes could not escape from the drive when released there. In the drive they would have six acres of woodland to hunt mice in and learn about the danger from a great horned owl. We had found an owl dead just outside the runs, killed possibly by flying into the fence when going for a fox, possibly by hitting the power line above the runs.

Next spring, Bold and Shy Baby again had two male cubs. After Josephine had gone and Napoleon had moved into the drive, we had opened up the division in the big run, so that they were all together. Nelson and Emma had one cub that year, an afterthought, whom we called "Emmarette." Shy Baby's cubs were named "Dancer" and "Bully Boy." They all, except Nelson, lived in one earth and Emma and Bold and Shy Baby shared the burden of feeding the cubs; Nelson would take no part in it.

We were worried about the in-breeding and now had too many dog foxes. The previous fall, Dr. Al Oeming, the well-known director of the Alberta Game Park, had come to our rescue and given us a complacent little vixen, whom we named "Alice" in his honour. She was given to Taffy and they now lived together in the run that we had built for Bold and Shy Baby, but which they had deserted. Alice and Taffy played together interminably all over the run but they were too young that year for breeding. Meanwhile, Tony had been put into the drive with Napoleon, and in the fall, when Dancer and Bully Boy were old enough to leave their parents, they were also put in the drive. That fall, the fall of 1976, was the Fall of the Great Escape.

The Rocky View District Council had decided to widen the gravelled road that ran past the game-park fence. This entailed moving the fence back twenty feet. We protested that they might let the moose out, but they said that they would first build a new fence and then remove the old one. We explained that the foxes would discover any new hole, but they assured us that they would leave no holes and agreed to pay compensation in the event of any fox escaping. The moving of the fence was left until late in the fall when Napoleon, Tony, Bully Boy, and Dancer were all in the drive. On the day that the fence was moved, they were joined by Taffy and Alice who had managed to bite through a strand of chicken wire in their run. Next morning only Alice and the foxes in the big pen remained. All the others had escaped through a hole that the men working on the fence had overlooked. Napoleon and Taffy returned after a few days freedom, but the others appeared to have gone for good. Early next spring, however, when Chris Harvey was coming through the drive gates, he saw a fox run under the culvert. It was bitterly cold, and the land still under snow. We opened the drive gates a little, having confined Napoleon in a new pen, and set the trap just inside the gates. Within an hour we had caught the fox, who turned out to be Dancer. He was in good shape having survived six months and the first half of a severe winter on his own.

In the spring of 1977, Alice and Taffy had three cubs, two dogs and a vixen. All the other foxes were excited about this event and showed great interest through the fences of their runs, but we had no other cubs. Emma and Nelson were now too old and arthritic for breeding. They spent most of their time underground and we only saw them occasionally on sunny days. Napoleon, who was supposed to be the same age, was as gay and as active as ever.

Bold and Shy Baby remained attached to each other. They played great games, chasing each other in the snow round and round the run, and sitting on top of the kennel, while they groomed each other. True to her name, Shy Baby always disappeared underground if we came into the run and had to be hungry before she reappeared to take food from Beryl. Bold Baby, the biggest and best looking of all the foxes (obviously aware of it) was confident enough to take food from her hand. All the foxes in the other pens treated Bold Baby as a superior, fawning and squirming to him through the fence, if he came near to them. Even Napoleon recognised his superiority. When the time for Shy Baby to have her cubs arrived, she disappeared underground for two weeks and then reappeared with nothing. We thought it possible that she had destroyed and eaten her cubs, as cannibalism is not unknown amongst foxes in captivity, but she had already raised two litters successfully in the same conditions of rather congested squalor. Although there was plenty of room in the run and several kennels and earths, she had seemed to have preferred the company of the older foxes, her parents.

This year Al Oeming gave us another vixen, whom we named Mrs. Newcome. Mrs. Newcome who was given a new run to herself was a very pretty, gentle fox. We decided to introduce Napoleon to her, caught him in the trap, and put him in Mrs. Newcome's run. He attacked her so furiously that we had to turn him out again. We decided to give Dancer to Mrs. Newcome. Dancer was living in the top half of the drive, Napoleon in the bottom half. Dancer appeared at feed times and carried his food away. Although Napoleon seemed to tolerate him near the house, it was never for long, and Dancer became progressively shyer. Unfortunately he was suspicious of the trap, and we were unable to catch him.

About Christmas, when the foxes were barking all night, and the time for pairing was once more upon us, we discovered fox tracks in the snow outside the runs and in the game park. We set the trap and caught a fine vixen in good condition. She was unafraid and waited tranquilly while I lifted up the trap so that Beryl could look underneath to sex her. We had only lost one vixen, Josephine. She had always been a friendly little fox, and this one was quite relaxed. In the unlikely case of it being a wild one, it would have been terrified. It must be Josephine, we decided. She had been away for two and a half years, for two breeding seasons, and had come back in search of a mate. We let her loose in the drive with Napoleon and Dancer, and in a few days they all disappeared. We found a hole in the rabbit wire that covered the gate, where we had neglected to put on the stronger wire.

Shortly after this Lil Larsen telephoned to say that there was a fox living under a shed just across the road from the drive gates. We found Napoleon there, sitting in the sun, with numerous fox tracks going under the building, the tracks of Josephine and Dancer. We fed them for a few days, and one night Napoleon returned, but Josephine and Dancer were gone. We hope that when the snow comes again we will be able to trace them.

The breeding season of 1978 was disastrous. We tried Napoleon with Emmarette, but they had frequent fights, and Emmarette spent her whole time trying to get back into the pen with her parents. This we eventually allowed her to do.

Napoleon then tried to dig through to Mrs. Newcome. We allowed him in, and there was another furious fight in which Mrs. Newcome was temporarily lamed. Napoleon had to be taken out again.

The spring was equally dismal as far as our foxes were concerned. Alice gave birth to two dead cubs before I was able to trap her and rush her to John Quine. John gave her a mild tranquilizer through the side of the trap, then managed to slip a noose over her head and pull her out so that I could hold her for his examination.

"She'd make a splendid subject for teaching a veterinary class" he said, looking up at me in his tough quizzical way, while his strong sailor's hands gently searched her stomach. "I don't know what I can do, she's so small isn't she? I can feel everything. The wall of her stomach is paper thin. Here is one. Just hold her up so that I can ease it out." A minute later a fine dead cub was lying on the table.

"Let's have another look," he said. "Yes. Here's another. Further back, this one." It too was soon on the table.

"Now she'll be all right," said John. "We'll just wash her out with a weak solution of penicillin and that ought to fix her. I don't think we've done any damage. I should let her rest in the trap for the night, and see how she is in the morning."

Alice slept quietly all night and most of next day. When she awoke I gave her a chick, which she ate with relish. In the evening I put her back in the run. She wagged her brush and squirmed when Taffy came to see her and next day they were playing together as if nothing had happened.

That season we had seen Bold and Shy Baby coupled and in due time Shy Baby disappeared for two weeks and again reappeared with no cubs. This was perhaps the nadir of our fox operation. We were to have setbacks, but we now heard that a postgraduate student from the Faculty of Environmental Design was going to commence a two-and-a-half year study of a release feasibility program for the swift foxes in which ours would play a predominant part.

Like Bison George, Bernie Carlington had come to Calgary University from McGill, and was slightly built and bearded. He gave an impression of efficiency and, unlike Bison George, who poured out his excitements, his troubles and his frustrations, Bernie went about his work in a quiet, reserved, and purposeful manner, like an abstemious priest walking through a beer parlour. Bernie Fox, as we soon called him, was usually well but appropriately dressed, as if for a part in a play. Sometimes he was studiously dishevelled in the fashion of students of his age. He favoured brightly coloured caps of the truck-driver style, and drove a red MG sports car.

Bernie Fox and Bison George had known each other at McGill and got on well together. They acquired a two-berth trailer which had a stove and sink from the university. It was moved into the aspens behind the house and connected to the house electricity and water. A good arrangement since they were not under our feet all the time. At first we thought that Bernie Fox was not really sympathetic to the foxes, regarding them only as objects for study, but he soon developed a genuine attachment. He also was conscientious with his studies, and I often looked out of my bedroom window, at any hour of the night, or in the early morning, to see him sitting in a chair in the fox pens, a night "scope" on a tripod in front of him or a pressure light burning at his side.

Under Bernie Fox's surveillance we tried Mrs. Newcome with three different mates. Napoleon was tried again and attacked her as furiously as before. Bernie Fox had to intervene and Napoleon was returned to the drive. We had already introduced one of Alice's last year cubs, whom we had named hopefully "Mr. Newcome." They would have absolutely nothing to do with each other, and only in wet weather would they share the same kennel. The other two of Alice's cubs had also been named. A young visitor had been asked to give a name to the dog and had called him "Harold." The vixen was named "Miz Alice." We tried Harold with Mrs. Newcome. They got on fairly well together but showed no affection, only sitting together in the sunshine, until he, like Mr. Newcome, climbed back into the big pen from where he was allowed to rejoin Taffy and Alice.

It is impossible to follow the changes in accommodation at this time. Miz Alice and Emmarette were living together in the west end of the big pen, Nelson in an earth in the middle and the Bold and Shy Babies in the east end. Taffy and Alice were together in their old run, which they shared with Harold, except for his brief visit to Mrs. Newcome. Mrs. Newcome was by herself in her own pen. Mr. Newcome was a floating lodger between Mrs. Newcome's run and the den occupied by Miz Alice and Emmarette.

Bernie Fox told us that he had not seen Miz Alice for a few days. Then Beryl discovered her amputated brush. We found nothing more of her and decided that she had been killed and eaten. As she got on well with Emmarette and her brother Mr. Newcome, our suspicious fell on Bold and Shy Baby, who were already suspected of unpardonable malpractice. A few days later, when Bold and Shy

Baby were spring cleaning, they pulled Emma's corpse out of an earth. She had been dead for some time. We knew that the vixens although not the dogs, will fight to the death, this was almost certainly a case of death from old age, because Bold and Shy Baby had always been gentle with the old foxes.

From now on things began to improve. Bernie made a new run below our bedroom windows, which included the peacock house with the plaster Buddha still sitting on top and the compost heap, which filled a square wooden frame.

Bernie Fox, like Bison George, found difficulty in identifying his charges. As he wished, at the time of their release to the wild, to fit them with radio collars, he decided to try out a collar, which might also help in identification.

Unfortunately, the first fox to walk into the trap was Alice, the one fox that anyone could recognize. Alice got a forefoot caught between her neck and the collar and hopped round on three legs, turning somersaults and throwing herself over backwards. She had to be caught again and the collar had to be removed.

Bernie Fox's next effort at marking the foxes for identification was to dye them with a vegetable dye used for colouring jellies. The dye was applied with a water pistol. Harold was the recipient of the first discharge and came out an ineffectual red. Bernie Fox's *tour de force* was with Emmarette whom he dyed bright green. Bernie, typically, had kept this to himself so that I was astounded one day to see a green fox flying through the aspens with Napoleon in hot pursuit. I do not know whether Napoleon was chasing her in anger, in curiosity, or in sexual excitement, but the hunt went on up and down the drive, until youth finally told in Emmarette's favour. Soon after that we caught her in a trap and put her in the new run with Mr. Newcome. They both settled down and seemed very happy together although it was a month before the green was all gone. Emmarette dug an earth under the compost heap of which she was extremely proud.

Mr. Newcome did not settle down at once to a comfortable married life. We saw him make several escape attempts, but each time to be defeated by the overhang. Early one morning, we found him in Mrs. Newcome's run, but when we opened the gate between Mrs. Newcome and Emmarette he came happily back to Emmarette. Next morning we discovered how he achieved this escape. The peafowl house has a half door which had been left ajar. Mr. New-combe jumped onto the top of this door and from thence onto the roof. There we saw him sitting with his back to the smiling plaster Buddha. He then descended a little way down the steep-pitched roof, then sprang lightly from the roof, over the gap between the house and the fence, and down into the other run. The door was closed and he has never been out since. In fact he and Emmarette are so settled down that although the gate of their run has been left open by mistake for a whole night, they could be found in the run by the morning.

Emma's death marked an end to the slump in our fortunes. Mrs. Newcome's run was enlarged to include the woodpile from which Napoleon, since he had the run of the whole game farm, was excluded. Mrs. Newcome cautiously explored the woodpile and then adopted it as her home. Harold joined her there and they paired up happily, while Mr. Newcome paired with Emmarette in an earth they made under the compost heap. Bold and Shy Baby were in the big run and Taffy and Alice in their own large run. Nelson went into his earth one cold night and never came above ground again. He had become very arthritic and died, in all probability like Emma, from old age.

CHAPTER 14

The Wild One

DURING THE SPRING of 1978 the Wild One stayed much by herself in the northwest corner of the game park. Sometimes we saw her early in the morning just as the sun touched the mountain tops to the west. Walking up the fence line towards the corner of the woods where she spent her day, she looked like a distant black puppet, silhouetted against the snow on the fields beyond. Sometimes she lay in the aspens, close enough to the road to be seen from a passing car. She now showed no fear of cars although one obviously had originally frightened her into the game park. Sometimes in the evening we caught a glimpse of her, browsing amongst the leafless willows at the edge of the aspens. For the most part we saw nothing of her; and at times it was such a long period that we began to hope that she had jumped out, as once she had jumped in.

"We've got to get her out," said Beryl. "I know that Petruska is upset. I can see that she is. Her place has been invaded first by the bison in the drive and now by this bloody moose. She must have been bred before she jumped in and now she's sure to have a cow as a calf. Probably twin cow calves. Then where will we be? We simply haven't got the feed for more than Petruska and Pollux."

I also was keen to get rid of the moose, although not so concerned about Petruska's feelings but because I was anxious about Beryl. In her daily peregrinations in search of Petruska at calving time, she might come upon the wrong moose, before the calf was active. Then she might find herself in trouble. One morning Petruska came to the house with a long scar on her side, from shoulder to flank. Something, which might well have been a moose's forefoot, had ripped the hair away, although the skin was only scratched. That was the end of tolerance as far as Beryl was concerned. She went off to telephone the Wildlife Service.

"They move bears out of parks, so there is no reason why they should not move a moose. She can be just as dangerous as a bear. Otherwise she will have to be shot," she said firmly.

A few days later an excessively confident young man arrived to discuss the removal of the Wild One. He worked for the Fish and Wildlife Service, which he hoped to join, and what he lacked in stature he made up in energy and enthusiasm.

Mitch, as he was called, suggested that if we could provide a couple of horses, he and a friend would bring a truck and they'd run the cow moose right down the fence line and into the truck. This was fighting talk, but instead of inspiring me with confidence it filled me with doubt. It was too near the time for calving for such violent action, and it was also too late for tranquilizing.

"It's all right," said Mitch, noticing my look of doubt, "I've worked in a racing stable. I can ride all right."

We now had Sarah Leete living in the log house, Betty and Chris having moved further afield. Sarah is a cool-eyed, slender-hipped girl, of strong character and decisive manner, an excellent horse-woman, and an expert skier. She was teaching riding and training horses. Apart from one or two horses under instruction, she had two of her own. One of these, El Cid, was a hunter type, who reminded me of a horse artillery wheeler. He was a horse of great character whom Sarah had rescued when he had one foot in the slaughter house. He was condemned because no fence could contain him, or if it did, he was intelligent enough to lift the gate off its hinges. The other was a tall palomino mare called "Tosen." She had been originally trained for dressage, a discipline that she detested, but had become instead an excellent trail horse.

I wasn't sure that Sarah would accept Mitch's qualifications without first seeing him ride. However, the necessity did not arise. After he had had a look at the terrain, he decided that it would not be so easy to haze the moose into a truck, nor to tranquilize her in the woods, owing to the difficulty of getting a truck to her. His next idea was to wait until the calf had been born and then to pick it up while it was still immobile.

"The problem will be finding the calf before it has started moving, without having the mother go for us. But if we could drive her off and then pick her calf up so that she would follow us, that might be the answer," said Beryl. From various experiences with Petruska we had considerable respect for an angry moose cow.

"If it is already active, we might run the calf with the horses until it drops and then pick it up," suggested Mitch.

Beryl, whose tender heart hardened when she thought of the Wild One upsetting Petruska, nevertheless did not like the idea of running the calf until it dropped, and neither did I. The Fish and Wildlife Service were starting a game farm at Ministic, and our visitor's thoughts were concentrated on the capture of the calf, while our aim was the removal of the mother. Eventually we agreed that as soon as we discovered the calf had been born, we would let the Fish and Wildlife Service know and see what they could do.

Six weeks later, Petruska failed to appear at the house for two days and when we had last seen her she looked ready to calve. "I'm going to find her," said Beryl.

"Right," I insisted, "I'll come with you with the Landrover and then, if you find the wrong moose, you'll have a refuge."

When we arrived at the place where Beryl expected to find Petruska we left the Landrover and set off, in different directions. We hadn't gone far before I saw a moose cow. It looked like Petruska, but I couldn't be certain.

"Here she is," I called to Beryl. "She's quite near the place where she chased Jerry Haigh round a tree. She's got a calf with her. I'm not sure which it is, but I think it's Petruska."

"You stay here," said Beryl, when she came up, "I'll see if she'll let me go up to her." She walked towards the moose, making a cautious approach, holding the bucket of feed in front of her. "Petruska. You are a clever girl, aren't you," she said. "Such a clever girl."

Instead of licking her lips in anticipation of the feed, the moose pinned back her ears and made a very ugly face.

"I should leave her," I shouted. "I don't think it's the right one."

Beryl came back reluctantly and we drove to the house, where we soon decided that it must have been Petruska after all, and that no two cows could look so much alike. We thought that she had been menacing only because I was near. Beryl went back by herself after lunch and found that it was indeed Petruska, who was very glad to see her. She finished the bucket of feed and the little calf, who turned out to be a bull, came up and sniffed her hand. As there had been a thunderstorm the day before, with the hail rattling on the roof, we called this calf "Thunder."

We saw nothing of the Wild One for two weeks. Again, it was in the early morning as she came up the fence from the pond, but this time she had a small brown calf behind her. The calf kept stopping to nibble at a leaf, or to wonder at the bright world around him, at a cowbird on the fence, or at one of the first red-winged blackbirds on the top of a willow bush. Then it dashed on in an excess of high spirits, passing its mother and kicking up its heels as it went. It was very active for so young a calf and was going to give us trouble if we tried to catch it.

Mitch at that time was unfortunately involved in a flood of abandoned calves. Several had been brought, and he was the only feeder and baby-sitter. The Wild One's calf was at least three weeks old when he telephoned that he was arriving with a truck and a tranquilizing gun and an expert, Doctor Bob Hudson. We were not sure where the Wild One was hiding but thought it probable that she was in the northeast corner. With the wind in the south she was well protected. To approach her from any other direction, the fence would have to be climbed, and the climber was liable to be discovered.

"Would riders be of any assistance?" I asked over the phone. Mitch thought that they would.

Mitch and Doctor Hudson arrived in a truck the same afternoon. The floor of the truck was about three feet off the ground so I wondered how on earth we were going to get a tranquilized moose inside. Doctor Hudson probably was wondering this also, but since we thought him to be the expert and he, as it turned out afterwards, expected us to be expert in this sort of thing, we did not press the point. We had to catch the moose first and a lot can be done with five people and blocks and tackle.

Sarah had arrived with El Cid and Tøsen, the palomino. I had once told her that in his old age the Duke of Wellington had to be put on his horse at Apsley House for his daily ride to the Horse Guards, where he was helped off it again. Now she told me that the Duke of Wellington's horse was ready and held her while I used a large stone as a mounting block and struggled into the saddle. We then disposed of cavalry and infantry in echelon, or with a refused flank, our shock troops — Doctor Hudson with the tranquilizing gun — advancing on the right, the infantry with the Datsun truck holding the centre, and Sarah and I on the left.

Doctor Hudson had hardly entered the trees when I saw the Wild One and her calf leave the far end of the wood and run along the road fence to the west. We turned her back twice, but she avoided Bob Hudson, and eventually she and the calf broke out separately near the stops in the centre.

"Where is Bob Hudson?" asked Beryl, coming up with Mitch.

"Doctor Hudson," he corrected her, unable to brook such lese-majesty even in the heat of action, but Bob Hudson was already away after the moose, and Sarah was long gone on a gallop across country in an attempt to turn it. Both the cow and the calf had disappeared towards the woods in the east, both going strongly so that we decided to call off the hunt. "She would have run right into me if I had not got out of her way," said Sarah, who had confronted her at the end of the pond dam.

For our next attempt to get rid of her I thought that, if only we could get her into the double fence, which led from the northwest corner of the game park to the gate at the southeast corner, we could drive her and the calf out of the gate, into country that the cow knew, for it was where she had come from.

A week later, we opened a gap in the bison fence, where it joined the road fence and tried again, this time with two more riders, Garry and Lilian Gingles, who were able to lend a hand. Using the same tactics as before, we soon had the cow and calf running along the inside of the road fence, and then, miraculously, through the gap and down between the two fences towards the gate in the southeast corner, where there was also a gate on the inner fence, the latter being shut and the other open. Beryl and the four riders met at the gap in the bison fence, scarcely able to believe that anything could have gone so easily. Leaving the others to close the gap, Sarah and I rode on between the two fences and, as we approached the pond, saw the cow moose and her calf trotting up the southern fence towards the gate. They presently disappeared over a rise. Rarely have I been more confident of success, but, as we approached the rise, we saw the calf running back to meet us. It stopped and doubled back out of sight, and as we trotted on there came the sound of the fence wire or the inner gate being rattled.

Sarah and I looked at each other in sudden doubt, which was soon to be confirmed. There were no tracks going out of the game-park gate, but tracks showed where the cow had jumped over the bison fence and back into the game park. The fence had been too much for the calf at first, but under pressure it had either got over the fence, an almost impossible feat for so small a calf, or it had squeezed under the gate which was set high on its posts to prevent a moose jumping over.

We tried again on several occasions, but never succeeded in getting the moose and her calf between the fences. Beryl's opinion of my scheme, which she began to regard as an excuse for a ride on one of Sarah's horses, fell lower and lower. Eventually she telephoned Jerry Haigh, the veterinarian who had come so promptly when Petruska was sick, and asked if he would come over again and tranquilize the moose, so that we could move her out. "At least he knows how to deal with wild animals," she said, with a pointed look at me.

I met Jerry again at the airport. He looked as if he had dropped whatever he had been doing in order to catch the aircraft. He was wearing a deerstalker cap, a battered quilted waistcoat, and jeans. He carried his tranquilizer gun and a box of darts and drugs and a handbag. "It may take us two days to get her," he told me.

That night we made our plans. We had left the horses in the game park for the past two weeks hoping that the moose might get accustomed to them and that it might even be possible for Jerry to shoot from the saddle, if the moose would allow the horses to get close enough. Although our own moose were getting used to them, the Wild One, who had been chased several times, continued to regard them with suspicion. We decided, therefore, to follow the same procedure that we had tried before. In order to prevent Petruska being tranquilized by mistake, Beryl had tied a yellow ribbon round her neck. This she had now worn happily for two days.

Next morning before breakfast, Beryl saw the Wild One going up the west fence, so that we at least knew roughly where she was. When Sarah arrived, we caught and saddled the horses. Then Jerry took up a position near the end of the dam where he could hide in some bushes and shoot if necessary at the moose as it left the dam bank, or if it ran below the bank between the fences. Beryl acted as a stop between the pond and the house and Sarah and I moved off to drive the moose out of the woods and along the fence. I had barely started into the woods before Sarah called that the moose had broken cover. Again the moose ran along the fence to the gap that we had made, then, instead of going through, turned down on the inside of the inner fence. Seeing Beryl acting as a stop, she and the calf continued down the fence, round the pound, and onto the dam, giving Jerry an easy shot as she left the dam. The dart, however, failed to penetrate properly, hung for a moment and then dropped out.

"I got her," said Jerry, recovering the dart as we got up to him, "but I'm not at all sure that she got a proper dose."

We all hurried on to the woods where we had seen her disappear, passing Martha and Mary on the way, standing close together, their pekinese eyes watching our movement, but appearing quite undisturbed. In the woods we found Pollux, Petruska, and Thunder who were interested but not alarmed by the horses. Petruska was wearing her yellow ribbon. We searched everywhere for the Wild One, crossing and recrossing the whole area, where Jerry thought she might be down. Although we saw the calf several times, we never found her, and eventually went back to the house for lunch. After lunch Jerry suggested that he might have a better chance of getting near her if he went by himself.

Later in the afternoon we heard the horn of the Landrover, and soon saw it coming across the country as if Jerry was once more in East Africa, with a rhino behind him.

"I've got her," he said, his face alight with enthusiasm. "I'll have to go back and keep her down, while you get something to move her. I've just got to get some more drugs from my box, and I think someone had better come with me as the bull may not let me near her."

"It wasn't Petruska by any chance?" asked Beryl, anxiously.

The light died momentarily in Jerry's eyes. "Well, I suppose it might be. But no. She wasn't wearing her ribbon. I took good note of that."

Beryl said she'd telephone John Stuart-Smith, to see if he could bring his fork lift, while I went with Jerry to check that the moose was not Petruska. Jerry and I drove back to where the cow moose was lying comfortably, head up, amongst the trees. As soon as I saw her grizzled nose I felt a pang of recognition, but there was no certain way of telling except by the notch in her left ear, where we had once unsuccessfully tried to affix a metal tag in order to comply with some bureaucratic regulation. She had pulled away and torn a small piece from her ear. She was not wearing a ribbon. I went up to her and took hold of her ear. The notch was there. She must have broken the ribbon against a branch since we had seen her in the morning.

Petruska looked as if she would happily stay where she was, but Jerry gave her the antidote for the drug that he had used and she got to her feet almost immediately, looking none the worse. As soon as Beryl heard of this mishap she hurried down with bread to comfort her beloved Petruska, who, directly she saw Beryl, came towards her licking her lips, and polished off the bread as eagerly as usual.

We continued the search for the Wild One but did not get near her again on that day.

Next morning we were off again, in good time but with reduced numbers since Sarah was unable to join us. I saddled El Cid, and with the palomino running free, made a sweep to the west. The Wild One and her calf were soon afoot and followed their usual route, but this time went through the gap in the bison fence and down between the fences. Jerry was in position near the end of the dam, and Beryl had driven the truck to the southwest corner in order to open the gate. She left the truck at the gate in the bison fence to act as a stop and stayed near it herself to ensure that the moose did not jump back over the fence as she had done before.

Jerry was positioned so that he could shoot at the moose through the bison fence, if she came between the fences, but he also had to be hidden from her if she came along the dam bank. He could not, therefore, put the muzzle of his gun through the fence, which runs along the top of the dam. If he hit her with a dart she would feel the effect before she got to the gate and would not be inclined to jump back into the park. It would then have been easy to move her and the calf out of the park. She gave him an easy shot as she trotted past, but the dart hit one of the wires of the fence and never reached the target.

Beryl heard some movement and then saw the moose running towards her on the other side of the bison fence. When only a few yards away she saw Beryl and the car, slid to a stop, then wheeled round and ran back in the direction that she had come from. Meanwhile, Jerry had reloaded and was showing a fine turn of speed in pursuit. He met the moose on her way back and she turned again and jumped over the fence back into the park, but he was close enough to get a good shot and the dart went home.

I found Jerry and Beryl standing by the fence. "I think we've got her this time," said Jerry. "We'll just give her a moment to let the drug take effect and then go and find her."

There were eighty acres of woodland to the north of where she had disappeared into the trees. We set off full of confidence that we would soon find her moving slowly under the effects of the drug. We searched and searched, for two hours perhaps, crossing and recrossing the ground where we thought she might be and were just about to call a halt when we put her up in a thicket. She was moving groggily, but still moving fairly fast. Jerry realized that he was going to need another dart. As he had not anticipated needing more than two, he and Beryl took the truck and drove back to the house to get one, leaving me to keep in touch with the Wild One. I soon picked her up again and followed her at a distance, fearing that if I pushed her she would get away from me in the thick cover. She was able to go through young aspen groves with comparative ease, where El Cid and I could only pick our way slowly since the gaps between the trunks were too narrow for the two of us, and El Cid had an "I'm all right Jack" attitude, which disregarded my knees.

Presently she disappeared into a thick grove so that I had to anticipate which way she would turn. I chose the wrong side and lost her completely. Beryl and Jerry took this disappointing news with equanimity, and we set off again in search of her. We were spurred on from time to time by a sight of the calf, but he had become separated from his mother. After another two hours, when Beryl and Jerry must have covered several miles on foot in rough going, we decided it was time to call a halt and went back to the house for food and a brief rest.

After lunch, thinking that perhaps the cow had gone back to the west side, I saddled Tøsen, the palomino and made my usual sweep to the west, before we went back again to search in the east side. This time El Cid was free and accompanied us, stopping from time to time to enjoy his independence and then cantering up to join us. The palomino was a lovely ride. She stepped carefully over deadfalls and went through narrow gaps between the trees and under low branches with greater consideration for her rider than the bluff and hearty El Cid. I found Pollux, Petruska, and Thunder but there was no sign of the Wild One. Petruska put her ears back, and El Cid lagged behind. I thought that he had decided to go home.

Tøsen and I had just come out of some thick cover and were moving in an open space of dead grass and bushes when Tøsen became alarmed and whirled round. There was the thunder of hooves behind us, and El Cid burst out of the trees at a gallop, looking like a charger who has lost his master, fleeing from the battle field. Close behind him and in hot pursuit came Petruska, closely followed by the monumental Pollux towering above us all. Tøsen had clear ideas of where she should be, and since she was eager to lead the flight, I allowed her to have her way. After a brief gallop we pulled up and found that Petruska had disappeared. Although El Cid may have thought differently, I do not think that Petruska attacked him—she was in estrus at the time and probably had been running from the bull (an important part of her "difficult to get" attitude in courting). Unhappily for El Cid, her route followed the path that he had just taken.

We were all pretty certain that the Wild One was still in the east side and after another long and tiring search Jerry said, "This is no good. I've got to leave early tomorrow morning, and if we don't get her today, we won't get her at all. We must have more people." Beryl went off to telephone our neighbours, an urgent cry for help.

They dropped whatever they were doing and came to our assistance: John, his dark eyed wife, Avki who was delighted to be doing something so unusual as helping to catch a moose, Lilian and Garry again, the latter on a big chestnut that, like Tøsen, had had no experience with cattle, let alone moose.

We formed a line and moved slowly down through the woods, on the east side until we came to the fence at the bottom, but saw only the calf. We had gathered in a disconsolate group, considering one more search to the west, when Avki said suddenly, "Isn't that a moose in the pond?" It was a moose, lying with only its head out of the water, looking towards us. It would have passed as a log up-ended, if it had not been for the two ears stretched towards us and Avki's sharp eyes. Jerry went off like a hound, running towards the dam bank near which she was lying. As he reached the bank she got to her feet and he was able to get another dart into her. The moose turned, floundered across the pond in the shallow water, and then took off towards the northeast, holding her head high and slightly crooked as she ran past us at her high stepping trot, with Jerry once more in pursuit.

"Keep her out of the woods," he shouted as he got near, and Garry and I riding on either side were able to head her from the trees, so that she continued in open ground towards the northeast corner. There we managed to turn her, just as Jerry arrived, still going at a good pace. He had gotten rid of his gun, his box of darts, and drugs to Avki and Lilian, choosing the youngest and the fleetest of foot, and they were following him at a surprising pace. "If you can hold her I'll bulldog her," he shouted, but the Wild One was not prepared to wait and turned back for the pond. Before she got there, Garry and I managed to stop her completely.

By now Jerry had covered a good mile over really rough going with Avki and Lilian, failing a little, but still panting in pursuit. Beryl said that we looked like some Norman tapestry with two mounted knights pursuing a deer, and with serfs running on foot. It only needed Sarah's two dogs (which would no doubt have been there if it hadn't been for the game fence) to complete the picture.

When Jerry arrived, he launched himself at the moose, catching her by the ears and wrestling her down onto her side. "She'll stay there" he said, "I'll just give her a tranquilizer," and turned to Lilian and his drug box. But the moose got to her feet again. By this time, John had arrived with the tractor and a rope. We were able to get the rope onto her, get her down again, and tie her. Then John moved the fork lift gently under her and lifted her up.

In a way, the operation had been successful. We had got rid of the moose without injury and to do so was the only alternative to having her shot, but it left rather a sour taste in our mouths. The best thing about it was the splendid help our friends so readily gave us.

When I was young, I loved all forms of the chase, particularly on horseback: in England with the hounds after a fox, in India after jackal, or after the fighting wild boar with a spear. But I rarely thought with compassion of the hunted. On this day I had felt again at least a trace of the old thrill, until, when trying to stop the moose, and hitting her on the nose with my cap, I saw that she was blind in one eye. That was the reason why she was carrying her head high and to one side, and had nearly run Sarah down on the dam. Now, we had to take a calf away from this poor, hunted, harried creature, bemused with drugs and blind in an eye. Instead of a feeling of jubilance at our success, I felt one of shame.

Happily, this story is not altogether a sad one. Some weeks later, we met Lilian, who told us that she had seen the Wild One, or at least a cow without a calf, so in all probability it was the Wild One, and that she was looking well.

As for the calf, he joined up with the others and became tame enough to come with them for their food. Recently when two years old, he was released to the wild, and I hope he will find his way into Banff National Park and be safe from the hunters.

CHAPTER 15

A Future for Foxes

THE LAST FEW YEARS our attention focussed more and more on the swift foxes. Partly because they are already extinct in Canada, and partly because of the difficulty of getting them to breed in captivity, they have presented the greatest challenge. Now that there were four compatible pairs showing every sign of being happily mated, Beryl and I felt like parents who, after a turmoil of divorce, desertion and disaster, at last know their children are happy and settled.

We were able to see Taffy and Alice coupling in broad daylight, and later Harold and Mrs. Newcome. Mr. Newcome and Emmarette were usually to be seen sitting close together and were obviously deeply attached to each other. We did not see them coupling, but I saw Mr. Newcome mount her in a disinterested way and then slip off without achieving anything. It was impossible to say whether he was an ineffectual spouse or whether he had been at it all night and wasn't feeling up to any more. Whatever the case, Emmarette appeared to be satisfied and, of all the vixens, looked the most pregnant.

The foxes' behaviour changed. They became much keener on their food, and the dogs, instead of gulping down their chicks so that they might steal from the vixens, now let the females have the first choice and occasionally offered them their own chicks. The most marked change was in Shy Baby, who for two years had been getting progressively more high strung. We had rarely seen her, except for fleeting appearances on sunny days, on the top of her den, or while hunting for the other foxes' forgotten morsels, just before dark. We had only to open the door, and she'd disappear immediately underground. For two months now, we had seen nothing of her at all and had left her food in the mouth of her den every evening.

In case Josephine was using the den in the drive, we left food there also. That some fox was using the den was obvious. A great deal of digging had been done, and after fresh snow there were always tracks going in and out. Beryl had a theory that only the vixens dig. I have never seen a dog fox digging, although I am reluctant to admit it lest she should compare my habits to theirs. After fresh snow there were also always at least two pairs of tracks going up to the drive gates, and a regular pathway going through the small hole left for the outside foxes in the gates by the house, which open into the game park. All over the game park, there were fox tracks, sometimes as far afield as the barn in the half-section. There was also fox tracks in the Larsen's place opposite the drive gates, leading under a shed, under the abandoned cottage, and into a stack of hay bales.

One day Beryl saw a strange swift fox coming down the drive. He crossed through the aspens and had a furious scolding match with Taffy through the fence of his run. He seemed to have no knowledge of chicks, when these were thrown to him and it was clear that he wasn't Napoleon, who was sitting on his den, near the back door. He was undoubtedly a male, because a female would never have behaved so aggressively to Taffy.

"I'm completely foxed," said Beryl. "It can only be Dancer. I hope he's living in the drive with Josephine."

"It might be Tony or Bully Boy, the ones the road men let out," I suggested.

In fact there was another fox in the drive, whom we were soon to recognize, and Josephine and Dancer were probably under the shack in the Larsen's place across the road.

We had just finished feeding the foxes, and the light was beginning to fade. I was looking from the window upstairs when I saw a fox titupping lightly down the road. It stopped near the house and I could see that it had very short ears and was in splendid condition, a beautiful swift fox.

"Here's Josephine," I cried in excitement to Beryl, but it wasn't Josephine. The fox passed under the window and I could see a slight crook at the end of its brush, the black tip being almost underneath. It was one of the few foxes that had an unmistakable identification mark. It was Shy Baby.

"But how on earth did Shy Baby get out?" asked Beryl. "Bold Baby's still inside isn't he?"

Shy Baby had never been a climber, although an ardent digger. When she had given birth to her first cubs, she had dug under the fence that divided the two runs in those days, and taken her cubs to her mother, Emma, to look after. As far as we knew, she had been there ever since. We could find no holes through the fence, and no long underground passages, leading to the outside. For some days we couldn't come up with an explanation as to how she had escaped, until I happened to see her with Bold Baby just outside the gate of the run, which we had left open so that Bold Baby might rejoin his mate. I opened the back door and threw them each a chick. They were not expecting my sudden appearance and took fright. Bold Baby slipped through the gate but Shy Baby launched herself at a point halfway up the gate and, with a wriggle, passed clean through the chain links, as if she had been a spirit fox. When I examined the gate, I found that the bison, trying to get through in the summer, had spread one of the links slightly. I had to examine it closely to see the difference. That was where she had gone through, and where she had left some foxy hairs to mark the spot. They slept by day either in the den in the drive or in their old den in the run. They didn't necessarily sleep together, but sometimes one curled up in the drive and one in the run, either in their country or the town house, as they preferred. Shy Baby lost her nervousness and once more took her food from Beryl by daylight and played in the run as she had in the old days.

The first three months of 1979 were normal for Alberta, that is to say snowy and cold. That is what one expects, but in March there were almost two weeks of summer weather when nearly all the snow disappeared. The gophers appeared on the roads and a few misguided robins in the woods. Bluebirds also misjudged their arrival, and ranchers who were busy with early calves, began to think of harrows and fertilizer. During these two weeks, I saw both a prairie falcon and a peregrine. They were flying with quick strong wing beats low over the ground as they followed the contours of the fields. They reminded me, by their speed and ruthless flight, of fighter aircraft, weaving low over the desert. The weather soon changed and we went back to winter, with snow falling interminably out of a gray sky.

On such a morning, I looked out of the window and saw Bold Baby off on a hunting expedition. He took the path towards the pond, then turned aside to pounce in the snow. After one or two pounces, which yielded no result, he continued his easy lope across the ice of the small pond just below the house. He stopped in the middle, ears pricked the west, then changed his mind and hunted back along the bank of the pond towards the east. Breakfast then took all my attention.

After breakfast Beryl called me to say that there was a fox or a small coyote coming back from the east.

"It's Bold Baby," she said, a moment later, "and he's got something in his mouth."

He loped past the front of the house, looking as free as the air and as graceful as a gazelle. He squeezed through the hole in the gate, cantered round the back of the house, and then trotted up to the den in the big run. There he called, first at one door and then at the other. Presently Shy Baby came out, squirming and lashing her brush. She took the mouse, that we could now recognize through the field glasses, from his mouth. Then she tossed it in the air, recovered it, shook it, and ate it. Bold Baby, the hunter, looked on with pride.

Soon after this we had a meeting with some of the members of the Wildlife Service and Doctor Hererro of Calgary University, who is in charge of the project to rehabilitate the foxes. All went well as far as the foxes were concerned. The study for their rehabilitation is to be continued, and the fence that encloses the game park was to be fox proofed, so that the cubs would have a wider range to learn self-preservation and to prepare themselves for release.

Some of our visitors were also interested in the bison and, for our part, we were particularly anxious to show them these animals in order that they might see how well they had done. Martha and Mary chose that day to disappear and came to the house neither in the morning nor in the evening. It was the first time that they had never appeared and, since they were again absent on the following morning, we went in search of them.

Presently we found tracks in the snow and after following them for some way we discovered two huge black mounds in the trees. In the previous year, they had grown enormously and tended to drive the moose away from their feed. Now Martha moved ponderously towards Beryl, and Mary towards me. They took a pellet from our fingers, with great dignity and gentility, curling their black tongues to receive it, like children taking a pill. Then they followed us, with funereal tread, back to the house, where they spent the rest of the day.

A few days later, on April 4, there was still no colour to relieve the drabness; the all prevailing grayness of the dull white snow and the dull white sky, the variegated grayness of the aspens and the dark spruce trees. Nothing living could be seen except a magpie sitting in a spruce tree just outside my window, his black and white coat matching the snow on the dark spruce bough.

Beryl and I had just returned from the drive. The drive den had been completely buried in snow, with only slight depressions showing at the entrances. If there were a fox inside, he hadn't been out for some time. Beryl had scraped away the snow from one entrance and put a chick and a piece of rabbit inside. I sat glumly at my desk wondering if the snow would ever stop. The only thing that had brightened the day had been the sight of a bald eagle, beating his way, low through the falling snow, towards the west. His white head and his white tail were difficult to distinguish against the matching sky.

In this disconsolate condition, I suddenly saw a fox come loping down the snow-covered drive, following the tracks of the truck that we had recently put away. It was Bold Baby, and he was carrying the piece of rabbit that Beryl had just left at the mouth of the den. He ploughed his way through the deep untrodden snow to Shy Baby's den and once more he called for her. Soon she came out, squirming and whimpering, to take the piece of rabbit from his mouth. No fox that behaved like Bold Baby could be an evil fox, and I felt my own spirit uplifted by their new-found freedom and happiness.

Even as I looked, I noticed that there was something different with the aspens. The catkins had broken out; small light gray tufts peeped from every varnished bud. These are the true messengers of spring. In a few days, there would be a swirl of wings as the wild duck returned to the pond. In a few weeks all the woods would be tinged with green, as the tender leaves began to brave the weather. Soon the vixens will disappear into their dens to have their cubs. Here, on the brink of the season of rebirth, I had intended to leave them, the little swift foxes, their future as a species still shadowy, but with small shafts of light beginning to illuminate the darkness.

But the foxes, in their typical foxy way have interfered, since good news cannot wait to be told. Between the four pairs, they have had fourteen cubs, only Mr. Newcome and Emmarette failing to produce live cubs, although they had some in the depths of the compost heap which didn't survive.

This morning as I looked out of the window, I saw Stuart (who is now back with us) sitting on the grass as cubs, now a year old, swirled around him like bees around a honey pot. They have the run of the whole game park now. One of them lifted a leg on Stuart's foot to mark him as its property. Stuart did not mind. Two or three have disappeared, either by escape or by falling prey to predators, but we still have three young vixens and plenty of males.

As for Martha and Mary, they now have a large and jealous buffalo bull, known as N'Komo. So let us wish them all good health, and a prosperous and fecund future.

About the Author

M iles Smeeton, the son of a Yorkshire country doctor, spent twenty years in the British Army, serving with distinction in India, North Africa, and Burma. As a young officer in India he met his future wife, Beryl Boxer, who had already travelled extensively, and usually alone, through Russia, China, Persia, and South America, often as a correspondent for *The Times.*

After the war, the Smeetons moved with their only daughter, Clio, then aged nine, to a farm in British Columbia. They stayed only briefly and spent the next twenty years living a nomadic life on their yacht the *Tzu Hang,* logging over 100,000 sea miles on the world's oceans. It was on a voyage around Cape Horn that Beryl had the experience of being washed overboard and then back on again.

In 1968 they purchased five hundred acres in the foothills of the Canadian Rockies, and they devoted the last twenty years of their lives to breeding endangered species and reintroducing them into the wild. They are credited with reestablishing swift foxes on the Canadian Prairies. Beryl died in 1979.

Miles Smeeton wrote nine books about his sailing days and his years on the Cochrane ranch. Adventurer, yachtsman, writer, and conservationist, he died in Calgary, Alberta, on September 23, 1988.